Hyena

Animal
Series editor: Jonathan Burt

Hyena

Mikita Brottman

REAKTION BOOKS

For David S.

Published by
REAKTION BOOKS LTD
33 Great Sutton Street
London EC1V 0DX, UK
www.reaktionbooks.co.uk

First published 2012
Copyright © Mikita Brottman 2012

All rights reserved

No part of this publication may be reproduced, stored in a retrieval
system or transmitted, in any form or by any means, electronic,
mechanical, photocopying, recording or otherwise without the prior
permission of the publishers.

Printed and bound in China

British Library Cataloguing in Publication Data
Brottman, Mikita
    Hyena. – (Animal)
    1. Hyenas
    I. Title II. Title
    599.7'43-dc23

    ISBN 978 1 86189 921 7

Contents

Introduction

The hyena, hermaphroditic self-eating devourer of the dead,
trailer of calving cows, ham-stringer, potential biter-off of
your face at night while you slept, sad yowler, camp-follower,
stinking, foul, with jaws that crack the bones the lion leaves,
belly dragging, loping away on the brown plain, looking
back, mongrel dog-smart in the face.
Ernest Hemingway, *Green Hills of Africa*, 1935

According to a keeper at the San Diego Zoo, people often
approach the striped hyena and, not knowing what kind of
creature it is, comment on the animal's beauty. But as soon as
they learn that the animal in front of them is a hyena, they
become critical and negative in their comments, and quickly
lose interest.[1] Why should an animal's cultural associations
have such a powerful impact on our feelings about it? In the
case of the hyena, so ingrained is the animal's reputation that,
upon learning its name, the creature itself is transformed before
our very eyes.

I first started thinking seriously about hyenas in 1992, after
seeing a 40-second British Public Information Film about the
dangers of car crime. In this short film, a pack of striped hyenas
runs up a dark alley laughing creepily and knocking over dust-
bins. They enter a public car park, swarm around a car and climb
on top of it. One of them sticks his head and neck through the
window and somehow manages to open the door. The hyenas
then go on a wild rampage, invading the car, tearing out the
stereo and ripping the upholstery. Finally, they run back down
the alley, laughing at the mess they've made. 'Today in Britain',
intones a serious male voice,

there's a type of scavenger. Like a hyena, it preys on the defenceless. It shows no compassion towards its victims. Most car crimes are committed by opportunists. If your car hasn't got adequate security, you're making it easier for them. Leave it unlocked, and they're laughing.

The final image was a road sign depicting a hyena with a red line through it, and the words: 'CRIME – together we'll crack it.'

This short film appeared regularly on British television in 1992, and I was oddly taken by it. I admired how the hyenas ran down the alley, like hooligans on a rampage. I was impressed by the way they tore into the sleek, expensive vehicle, pulling it apart with their teeth, strewing the contents of some middle manager's briefcase all over the ground. I was all in favour of this gleeful assault on the symbols of executive privilege. To put it bluntly, I was on their side. Yet, I was in the minority. Apparently, the film was unusually successful in combating car theft, particularly when coupled with the nationwide police initiative targeting car criminals known as 'Operation Hyena'.

At the time, I did not know enough about hyenas to understand how this short propaganda film exploited their public image as criminals and thieves. The voiceover described the hyena as 'a type of scavenger' that 'preys on the defenceless', but, as I have since discovered, not all hyenas are scavengers, and what is more, scavengers do not 'prey on the defenceless', they eat corpses and carrion. To make matters worse, the hyenas shown in the film run together in a pack, laughing – and yet these are striped hyenas, which are not pack animals and do not laugh. In fact, striped hyenas are cautious, gentle creatures that generally live alone or in pairs.

I have since learned that this 'public information' film is typical in its presentation of hyenas as filthy, snickering tricksters lurking in the back alleyways of the animal kingdom. Indeed, throughout history, these fascinating and unusual creatures have been scorned, demonized, reviled, mistreated and misunderstood, miscast as scapegoats, scavengers, vandals and thieves. More often than not, this unloved animal becomes a projection of the observer, representing whatever kind of Otherness is felt to be most frightening. In other words, our hyenas are ourselves.

Those familiar with real hyenas do not find them unappealing. Zoologist Hans Kruuk, author of *The Spotted Hyena* (1972), believes 'there is a magic about hyenas', and those who spend time with them cannot help but 'fall for the spell' of these animals that are 'so totally different'.[2] Get to know a hyena up close, and you will encounter a fabulous, enchanted beast, neither cat nor dog but an odd combination of the two, related more closely to cat than dog, with a touch of the ferret thrown in for bad luck. There is a sublime and hideous grandeur to this big-eared, red-eyed, corpse-eating creature that has rarely been recognized or acknowledged. In this book, I would like to introduce you formerly and properly to the hyena. I hope you will meet a new friend.

1 Evolution and Distribution

In one fantastic form or another, the creature we now call the hyena has been around for more than 26 million years. Its earliest ancestor was a small, nimble, tree-dwelling mammal resembling a streamlined badger, with short, dense fur and a striped or spotted pelt. Over millions of years, these agile creatures adapted to their environment by increasing in size, growing longer legs and coming down from the trees, finally evolving into dog-sized carnivores. Fifteen million years ago, over 30 different species of these proto-hyenas roamed unchallenged through Europe and Asia. Their reign came to an end between five and seven million years ago, when lowered sea levels exposed the Baring Land Bridge. Consequently, large numbers of other canids – including wolves, foxes, jackals and coyotes – crossed overland from North America to Europe and Asia, vastly outnumbering the hyenas and wiping out their food supplies. Only two types of hyena survived: one that adapted by eating insects, and a second that developed bone-crushing teeth. These are the ancestors of the hyenas that live among us today.

Their incredible teeth turned the early hyenas into scavenger kings, able to take advantage of all the scraps left over from the kills of sabre-toothed tigers and other animals that were once their rivals and competitors. As a result, three million years later, hyenas were flourishing again. Nine species thrived at this

time, including the mega-scavenger *Pachycrocuta*, a giant beast that weighed up to 113 kg (250 lb) and could crush elephant bones with its teeth. These nine species prospered until the sabre-toothed cats were replaced by smaller, short-fanged felids that ate more efficiently, leaving fewer scraps and bones. Over time, hyenas adapted again, learning to hunt for themselves, and the Hyaenidae family evolved into the four species we know today: the Spotted Hyena (*Crocuta crocuta*), the Striped Hyena (*Hyaena hyaena*), the Brown Hyena (*Hyaena brunnea*) and the Aardwolf (*Proteles cristata*). Today, all four types of hyena may

Prehistoric hyenas, reconstructed from fossil records: the primitive, civet-like *protictitherium*, the running, dog-like *hyaenotherium*, and *adcrocuta*, a more 'modern' species.

Hyenas with erroneous binominal names: Aardwolf *(Proteles lalandie)*, striped hyena *(Hyaena striata)*, brown hyena *(hyaena brunnea)* and spotted hyena *(hyaena crocuta)*, 1902.

be found in the arid and savannah zones of sub-Saharan Africa. The brown hyena has the most limited distribution; the striped hyena is rare, too, but may also be found in areas of North Africa and Asia. The spotted hyena is adapted to less arid conditions, but inhabits the greatest variety of habitats and, numerically, is Africa's dominant large carnivore.

Some say they look like a cross between a cat and a dog; others describe them as a mixture of wolf and fox, but hyenas actually belong to the Herpestidae family – the family of mongooses and meerkats (nearer to cats than dogs, but not especially close to either). The hyena's closest relatives are not, as one might imagine, the jackal or the African wild dog, but the mongoose, the meerkat and the banded palm civet. All four species of hyena share certain characteristics. They all have an odd, skulking gait, due to the fact that their hind legs are quite a bit shorter than their front legs. The ears are large in proportion to their bodies, either pointed or round, and radiate heat. They have sloping, muscular hindquarters, brown, striped or spotted pelts, and very distinct manes down the middle line of the neck and back, which stand on end during confrontations. Notably, the three carnivorous species of hyena have massive jaws in relation to their body size; these were accurately described in an unusually sympathetic discussion of the hyena that appeared in *Harper's New Monthly Magazine* in 1854. The creature's jaws, we are told, 'are possessed of enormous strength and adapted for crushing the hardest substances; the muscles which raise the lower jaw are in consequence unusually developed, and appear like enormous masses of flesh on either side of the head'.[1] The front teeth are used for killing, holding and biting, while the molars and pre-molars are used to crack and crush bone (unlike dogs' teeth, which work the other way round). Hyenas also have a powerful stomach system that lets them digest parts of the prey no other animal can consume, including teeth, large bones and even hooves. Anything left over is excreted in their faeces, which are usually wet and light green with a texture like clay, eventually drying to powdery white lumps because of the large amounts of calcium they contain. Incidentally, hyena faeces also make very

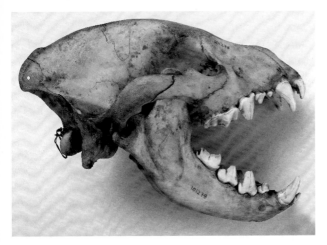

Hyena's skull with mouth open, showing its powerful teeth.

solid fossils. In early 2009 a team of researchers excavating Gladysvale Cave, near Johannesburg, South Africa, discovered five human hairs in fossilized hyena dung that dates from between 257000 and 195000 years ago.

Only the spotted hyena 'laughs', but all hyenas are vocal. Although their distant whoops and howls resound eerily through the still desert night, most of their calls are soft, and are used only among family members and close friends. Some unusual sounds in the hyena repertoire include a long-distance cackle and an affectionate cooing noise, but most of their vocalizations fall into one of two categories: yips and whoops. Mood and rank within the social hierarchy are indicated by visual displays of dominance (bristling mane, erect tail and ears, hunched back, growling) and submission (presenting the anus and genitals, flattening the ears, grimacing and licking the lips). Hyenas will often mock-fight and muzzle-wrestle, grabbing one another's manes or lower jaws between their teeth. When fighting, they protect their back legs by dropping their hindquarters to the ground.

All species have scent glands that open into the rectum just inside the anal opening, where they store a thick, sticky secretion used to mark territorial boundaries. This pouch is turned inside out during scent marking, with the hyena crouching down to leave deposits of 'butter' on grass and sticks. This is known as 'pasting', and in spotted and striped hyenas it is usually followed by the animal scratching the ground with its forepaws like a dog, to spread the scent around. Pasting can occur at any time and place, but is especially marked close to the den, around a kill and when lions are present.

Also known as the laughing hyena, the Spotted Hyena (*Crocuta crocuta*) is the largest, best known and most widespread of all four species. Distinguished by their short, spotted fur and uncanny cackle, spotted hyena can be found all over Africa south of the Sahara, with the exception of the Congo basin. Their pale brown fur is short and rough, with a woolly undercoat, and a dark brown mask covers their face and legs. Spotted hyenas have one of the richest vocal repertoires of any terrestrial mammal, including primates. They communicate through a series of high-pitched whoops, grunts, yips, affectionate murmurs and whines, as well as their well-known laughter (actually an expression of excitement and frustration) through whose pitch and tone they convey information to each other about social status, mood, desires and age (the older the animal, the higher the pitch). Clans, which vary in size from 5 to 90 members, usually settle in the abandoned lairs of warthogs, springhares, jackals and other animals, though adults will generally sleep

Spotted hyena
taking a stroll.

Karl Joseph Brodtmann, 'Spotted and Striped Hyenas', lithograph from Heinrich Schinz, *Natural History and Images of Man and Mammals* (1840).

Gefleckte Hyäne.   Hyéne tachetée.

Gestreifte Hyäne.   Hyéne rayée.

in the open, beside dense shrubs, lakes, streams or mud banks. Cubs from different litters are brought together and nursed in a communal den until they become sexually mature at around three years of age, at which point males leave the clan and seek partners elsewhere.

Spotted hyena clans are governed by a strict ranking system in which, significantly, the females are dominant. Female spotted hyenas, weighing an average of 65 kg (145 lb), are larger and far more aggressive than the males. An alpha female rules the clan and females (including female cubs) get first servings at the kill, while males wait patiently on the sidelines. Zoologists believe this female dominance is adaptive, and has evolved due to the fact that, in order to develop their huge skulls and bone-crushing jaws, cubs need to nurse for at least a year (their mother's milk contains more protein than that of any terrestrial carnivore, and more fat than the milk of any animal except the polar bear). In the later stages of pregnancy, moreover, hyena mothers are flooded with high levels of androgens, including testosterone. High-ranking mothers give their cubs more hormones than low-ranking mothers, so the cubs of dominant females are more aggressive and sexually active than cubs of the lower ranks, and are given first priority at a kill. Spotted hyena hierarchy is nepotistic – cubs of the dominant females automatically outrank all other hyenas, including adults, whatever their size, though these top-ranking cubs can lose their 'titles' when their mother dies.

This injection of androgen builds up the offspring's powerful jaws and hindquarters and also promotes dominant and aggressive behaviour. When they are born, these vicious nippers are the largest of all carnivore cubs in relation to their mother's weight, weighing around 3 kg (7 lb), and they arrive ready for trouble, with canines, incisors, and eyes wide open. Inevitably, the aggravation begins the moment they arrive in the den, and a quarter of spotted hyena cubs are victims of their litter mates' violence. Since male hyenas provide no assistance at all in rearing their young, and since cubs this tough obviously need to be kept in line, female spotted hyenas must be remarkably tough.

The cubs are born with soft, black fur and – in some respects – grow up very quickly. At one month, they are already ritually sniffing each other, marking out their territory and running at high speed. A couple of months later, they lose their black coat and grow spotted, light brown fur. By eight months, they are starting to hunt, and at one year old, they are already running with the pack. However, in order to develop their powerful jaws and tough skulls, the cubs take almost eighteen months to wean from the breast. No wonder their mothers need to wear the trousers.

More than the trousers, in fact – female spotted hyenas also sport a 20-cm-long (8-in) clitoris that is the same size and shape as the male's penis, accompanied by a pair of pseudo-testes. In the centre of this appendage is an opening leading to the vagina. Prior to copulation, this appendage grows erect, pointing downwards. For intercourse to occur, the male hyena needs to stoop down low enough to insert his erect penis into the end of the female's erect clitoris; to do so, he needs to be almost standing upright on his back legs, clutching the female's rump. As one might imagine, this is a tricky business. Under such circumstances, passive, calm males tend to have more success than those who are jittery, nervous or aggressive, so male hyenas are always craven and submissive when approaching females, even on those rare occasions when the female is smaller than they are. With enormous pain and difficulty, the female spotted hyena gives birth to her cubs through this cliteriform appendage – two or three at a time. So painful and dangerous is this birth process that one in five mothers does not survive the first litter, and even if the mother survives, the cubs are often stillborn, although the tearing and stretching of the clitoris makes subsequent deliveries much easier.

Hyena experts widely believe that this penis-like clitoris in the female hyena is a side effect of the elevated androgen production

in the womb. It appears that this clitoris was subsequently maintained and elaborated as an adaptive trait because it proved useful as a way of signalling status; the more erect the pseudo-penis, the more subordinate the status. By displaying their submission to dominant females, subordinate females may thereby improve their chances of survival and eventual reproduction. Moreover, with such an appendage, female hyenas can never be coerced into sex, which would lead them, albeit temporarily, to cede their dominance to a male. Instead, female spotted hyenas carefully vet their sexual partners, and their first choice is always an immigrant to the pack (as this discovery was reported on one blog, 'hyena gals prefer suave foreigners to boy next door'[2]). This explains why 90 per cent of male hyenas leave their birth clans. By rejecting their clan mates, females avoid inbreeding and help to maintain the genetic health of the pack.

Unsurprisingly, the female spotted hyena's genitals are a source of fascination among scientists, and can lead to awkward moments on safaris and nature shows, which might be one of the reasons why these remarkable creatures are rarely found in zoos. People seem to feel uncomfortable at the idea of female genitals that are larger than the male's, especially when they grow visibly erect and engorged. The nudging, winking voice-over that accompanied a recent show about spotted hyenas on the National Geographic Channel is typical. 'The head of the clan swaggers past, bristling with testosterone. Its penis swings low and proud', we are informed, over footage of a spotted hyena sporting what appears to be a large erection. 'With its confident rolling gait, this is one cocksure killer. But this well-hung hunter has a secret. He is a She! This is the queen of the swingers. Her huge member, which many males would be proud to bear, is in fact a clitoris.' When spotted hyenas come to mate, we are warned, archly, 'two penises are on a collision course, and it's easy to cock it up'. These sniggering double entendres, unchar-acteristic of an authoritative science show, seem designed to cover a fundamental embarrassment in the face of this 'mistake of nature'. Equally embarrassing is the fact that zoo personnel often find it impossible to distinguish the male of the species from the female, although trained zoologists can readily tell the difference. In July 2007 there were some red faces at Monarto Zoo south-east of Adelaide, Australia, when a 'male' spotted hyena, after spending time in quarantine with another male, 'unexpectedly' gave birth to a cub.

Spotted hyenas have long been misrepresented as cowards and scavengers, when in fact they are among the most abundant and successful carnivores in sub-Saharan Africa, with a better kill rate than lions. They hunt in packs of ten or fifteen, led by the alpha female, eventually breaking up into smaller groups of two or three. These groups call to each other with a special whooping sound when prey is sighted – usually gazelle, wildebeest, water buffalo or zebra, but sometimes young giraffes, rhinos or hippos. Spotted hyenas have also been known to prey on farm animals, including horses, donkeys, camels, poultry and even cats and dogs. Living up to their reputation, however, they will sometimes scavenge from human camps and – more and more often, particularly in South Africa – from dumps and landfills.

When hyenas attack, their chase is usually rather slow, and initiated by one animal, with the rest of the clan joining in when necessary. The prey is eaten alive, and jackals will sometimes congregate at the kill, though they will be chased off if they come too close. The kill itself, according to hyena authority Joanna Greenfield, is cruelly spectacular.

> They hunt in large, giggling groups, running alongside their prey and eating chunks of its flesh until it slows down through loss of blood, or shock, or sheer hopelessness, and the hyenas grab for the stomach and pull the animal to a halt with its own entrails or let it stumble into the loops and whorls of its own body.

Spotted hyenas, she writes, 'are the sharks of the savanna'.[3]

THE STRIPED HYENA

The Striped Hyena (*Hyaena hyaena*), also known as the Barbary hyena, is smaller than his spotted cousin, with a thick, heavy-set

Striped hyena.

body that weighs between 25 and 55 kg (60 and 120 pounds) and measures 1.2 to 1.5 m (4 to 5 ft) from snout to tail. The body and legs are covered in coarse grey fur with vertical black stripes that turn lighter in the summer, and the face and muzzle are dark with a black throat patch under the neck. From nape to rump, a thick mane covers the back; this can be raised up in a threatening display that is especially prominent between the shoulders, on the dorsal crest. The legs are long and striped, and the tail is black, white and bushy.

Striped hyenas may be found over much of North Africa and across the Middle East and Pakistan, into the Arab Peninsula and all the way to eastern India and parts of Turkey. Striped hyenas sometimes live in groups like their spotted relatives, but they may also live alone or in pairs. Unlike spotted hyenas, striped hyenas are nocturnal, sometimes territorial and sometimes nomadic, living in open country and deserts, though rarely more than six miles from a water hole. They can also be found in the forests and along the coastal shores of India, where they feed on the bones of corpses washed up from the ocean.

Their main diet is carrion and the leftover kills from other predators, and they will often dig shallow holes with their paws in which to hide bones, flesh and meat. However, striped hyenas are quite omnivorous, and also prey on mammals like wild boar, porcupine and tortoise. In addition, they will eat insects, vegetation and fruit, and are considered to be pests by many farmers and herdsmen, since they sometimes kill farm animals and raid fruit plantations.

These shy creatures hunt at night, mostly in solitude. Although striped hyenas of the same sex are seldom close, those of the opposite sex will habitually groom, nuzzle and otherwise enjoy one another's affections. A female striped hyena reaches sexual maturity between two and three years of age and her oestrous cycle is about seven weeks long, only one day of which is she actually fertile. She can come into heat at any time of the year, and remains pregnant for about thirteen weeks, usually giving birth to a small litter, of which, in general, only two survive. The young open their eyes from five to nine days after birth and start eating solid meat at thirty days, though they will continue to nurse for four to five months. The den is usually in a hole or crevice in between rocks, and the home territory will be marked by scent from the anal glands.

Striped hyenas do not 'laugh', and have a significantly lower range of vocalizations than spotted hyenas; in fact, most of their greeting rituals and long-distance communications take the form of scent marking. While they have no natural predators, they are sometimes killed in conflicts with wolves or crocodiles, and are often trapped and poisoned for preying on livestock or raiding farms. Like spotted hyenas, they have also been known to kill humans, though such incidents are rare. Zoologist Joanna Greenfield, herself the survivor of a striped hyena attack, tells the story of a young boy in Nairobi who, watching

Jean-Charles
Werner, 'Striped
Hyena', from
Isidore Geoffroy
Saint-Hilaire,
*General and
Particular History of
Organizational
Anomalies in Man
and Animals*
(1832–7).

over a herd of goats, fell asleep leaning on his stick and became a victim of this normally reticent predator.

> A hyena appeared and opened the boy's stomach with one quick rip. For the hyena it might have been play, this trying on of assault. But he won, as he was bound to do. I was told that someone took the boy to a doctor and he died a while later . . . I would have liked to ask him what he saw in the hyena's eyes.[4]

According to the author of the anonymous 1854 article in *Harper's New Monthly Magazine*, 'it has been asserted that the striped hyaena is of a less ferocious temper than his spotted brother', but, adds the author, judiciously, 'we can hardly think that this can really be a fact . . . We believe the spotted hyaena is to the full as susceptible of kindness, and amenable of education, as is the other variety.'[5]

The most rare of the four types is the Brown Hyena (*Hyaena brunnea*), sometimes known as the strand wolf in reference to the prominence of this species on the Strand of the Western Cape in South Africa. The brown hyena is distinguished by its shaggy brown coat reaching down to the belly, striped legs, long, pointed ears, light brown mane and bushy tail. The head and snout are dark brown, the forehead black, and the legs are brown with white stripes. The overall size is about the same as that of the striped hyena.

Brown hyenas are found primarily in southern Africa, mainly in Namibia, Botswana, western and southern Zimbabwe and southern Mozambique. Like spotted hyenas, brown hyenas are social animals, though like striped hyenas they are primarily scavengers that forage alone and do not maintain a territory. Brown hyenas are mostly nocturnal, and males help to raise the cubs. As with the spotted hyena, the male brown hyena will leave the clan and join another group when he is fully grown. The females come into heat many times during a single breeding season, and typically produce their first litter in their second year of sexual maturity, giving birth in hidden dens far from the reach of lions. Usually, only the dominant female breeds, producing a small litter every twenty months, but if two litters are born in the same clan, the mothers will nurse each other's young. Brown hyena cubs weigh around 1 kg (2.2 lb) at birth, open their eyes after about eight days, and leave their dens at three months, but they are not fully weaned for another ten months or more, and stay close to home. The cubs do not fight in the way spotted hyena cubs do – in fact, they will often help one another out, with the older cubs guarding the younger.

Brown hyenas are mainly scavengers, foraging alone from carcasses killed by larger predators, though they also eat insects, eggs and fruit, especially melons. They sometimes catch small mammals like hares, lambs and foxes, and although their powerful sense of smell allows them to scent a kill upwind several miles away, they are, in general, rather poor hunters. Other than at dens, brown hyenas are usually seen on their own, at night, while foraging for food (they travel on average around twenty miles each night). Black-backed jackals have been observed following brown hyenas to scavenge the food they drop or leave behind (yes, some scavengers have scavengers of their own), but the jackals need to be discreet to avoid being eaten. Otherwise, live prey is a very small part of their diet except for those hyenas that live in the southern coastal Namib

Brown hyena at a water hole.

Brown hyena carrying the skull and spinal column of a kudu.

Desert, which regularly prey on Cape fur seal pups. As a result of the latter, there is a high density of brown hyenas along the Namib Desert coast, where seal breeding colonies play a major role in their sustenance. The hyenas will visit these colonies on their foraging trips to feed on fresh carcasses or to kill the pups, which are available all year round, since a seal pup is only weaned shortly before the next pup is born. Periods of food shortage are therefore rare and the brown hyenas of the Namib Desert coast are in an especially good condition.

Elsewhere, however, brown hyenas are often shot on sight by farmers who mistakenly blame them for the death of their cattle. They are also illegally snared and poached for their fur, and the brown hyena is eaten by Kalihari bushmen, though the spotted hyena is not. What is more, the gradual erosion of their habitat – often a result of diamond mining – has led to the brown hyena being listed as an endangered species. Currently, the total population size of brown hyenas is estimated to be between 5,000 and 8,000 animals, which makes them one of the rarest large African carnivores. Until recently, there was no interest in preserving the species, which was widely considered to be 'too ugly' to attract any attention. Fortunately, the Brown Hyena Research Project, based in the Namibian desert, is currently studying the ecology of this unique species with an eye to preservation.

THE AARDWOLF

Last, but certainly not least, is *Proteles cristata*, the Aardwolf ('earth-wolf' in Afrikaans), the least typical of the hyena family in that its diet is restricted to termites. The aardwolf resembles a much smaller version of the striped hyena, and never weighs more than 14 kg (30 lb). In earlier days, the aardwolf was considered by some zoologists to be a mere mimic of the striped

Aardwolf postcard and stamp, Eritrea.

hyena and was separated into a family of its own (Protelidae), but this hypothesis has now been dismissed. Instead of some other beast 'disguised' as a hyena, the aardwolf is now considered a card-carrying member of the hyena clan.

Although significantly smaller, the aardwolf resembles both brown and striped hyenas in its large, pointed ears and long, erectile mane, which extends from behind the head, down the middle of the back and on to the bushy tip of the tail. The long, slender muzzle gives this gentle creature a foxy look. The fur is a rusty fawn colour with regular black stripes; the legs, also striped, are long and thin; and the front feet have five toes, unlike those of the other hyenas, which have four.

A nocturnal creature, the aardwolf is native to north-eastern and southern Africa and lives almost exclusively on the savannah,

'Aard Wolf, Brown Hyena, Spotted Hyena and Striped Hyena', from *Johnson's Household Book of Nature* (1880), chromolithograph.

where termites can be found. The southern population ranges over most of South Africa, extending into Angola, southern Zambia and south-western Mozambique, while the northern population extends from central Tanzania to north-eastern Uganda and Somalia, and through Ethiopia and Sudan to south-eastern Egypt.

Young aardwolves live quietly in monogamous pairs with their young, sleeping in underground burrows by day and foraging alone at night, although they become more diurnal in the winter months, huddling in their dens at night to conserve energy. Rather than digging for food, the aardwolf licks termites off the soil surface; it therefore lacks the well-developed claws and limbs of other ant-eating creatures. Consequently, although they are capable of digging their own dens, aardwolves generally use the abandoned borrows of aardvarks, porcupines or spring-hares. The entrance to the den, usually below ground level, leads to a passage which, in turn, narrows down to a small, oval-shaped tunnel big enough only for the cubs (not adult hyenas or other large carnivores, such as lions) to enter.

The aardwolf is the only non-carnivorous member of the hyena family, which accounts for its relatively small size. Aardwolves feed almost exclusively on insects, mostly termites and larvae. Their teeth are reduced and adapted for termite eating, and they have long, sticky tongues for licking up bugs. When a termite mound is discovered, the aardwolf will take care not to eat all the termites, leaving enough for them to rebuild the colony; then, months later, it will return for a second helping. The aardwolf will occasionally eat other insects, larvae and eggs, but does not scavenge or kill larger animals.

Interestingly, aardwolves live in similar areas to aardvarks ('earth-pigs' in Afrikaans) and will sometimes feed from termite mounds that aardvarks have excavated. Like the striped and brown hyenas, the aardwolf is generally silent, except under stress, when it will threaten enemies with a soft clucking sound. During fights and chases, the mane will become erect, but if only threatened slightly, the aardwolf will simply fluff out the hairs of its tail, a gesture also used by cubs at play.

Young aardwolves spend their first six to eight weeks in the den, then begin supervised foraging, and are usually independent by the age of four months, though they generally remain 'at home', in the same den as their mother, until the next litter arrives. Aardwolves are plentiful in population, since farmers generally consider them useful and leave them alone. In some areas, however, they are killed for their fur. Other threats come from dogs and from the poisons that are now regularly sprayed on the land to destroy insects. Aardwolves are plentiful in zoo populations, where, although their nocturnal habits often confound visitors, they tend to live long and healthy lives. The record lifespan for an aardwolf in captivity is fifteen years, in East London Zoo, South Africa.

2 The Hyena and Human History

> But scanty favor has this ill-favored, unhappy-looking
> quadruped met with hitherto in the eyes of zoologists; and
> as a general rule, it will be found that the older the work on
> natural history in which he is mentioned, the more abundant
> are the hard epithets lavished upon his devoted head.
> 'The Hyena', *Harper's New Monthly Magazine*, 1854

The hyena has always been a mystery to us. From ancient times,
this fearful creature has lurked on the fringes of human culture,
rarely taking centre stage, always shrouded in a dreadful confusion. Other scavengers – the jackal, for example, and the vulture
– are sometimes allowed a distant nobility, but the hyena has no
saving grace. It is a liminal beast surrounded by taboos, both
reviled and revered, both sacred and profane.

Where to begin? Perhaps the best place to start is with the
hyena's zoological classification, which has always been both
confused and confusing. It is thought that the spotted hyena
conforms to the *chaus* described by Pliny the Elder, as well as to
the *crocotta*, which the Greek scholar Strabo identified as a wolf-
dog hybrid. In his *Geography* (*c*. AD 18), Strabo refers to the
hyena as a 'cameleopard' and notes that its hindquarters are so
much lower than its forequarters, so that it always appears to be
sitting.[1] In the twelfth edition of his *Systema naturae* (1797),
Linnaeus classified the *chaus* as part of the cat tribe (*Felis chaus*),
placing hyenas into the genus *Canis*, between wolves and foxes,
despite the fact that in 1756 French zoologist Mathurin Brisson
had already given the form a generic distinction under the
name *Hyæna*. In the thirteenth edition of Linnaeus' *Systema naturae*, the German naturalist Johann Gmelin gave the spotted
species the name *Canis crocuta* (1788), though Thomas Pennant,

Hyena depicted in a Roman mosaic found in Tunis, Tunisia, 1st to 2nd century AD.

in his *Synopsis of Quadrupeds* (1771), had previously described it under the title *Hyæna* and placed it under the category of *Spotted Hyænas*. Georges Cuvier, in *The Animal Kingdom* (1817), claimed there were at least two different species of spotted hyena, based on regional differences in coat colours. However, subsequent naturalists did not accept this, for although coat variations were noted, the differences were not considered significant enough fully to warrant classing them as different species. In his *Zoological Miscellany* (1831), John Edward Gray brought the spotted hyena under the Felidae, placing it within a category including other hyenas and the aardwolf, where it has remained, more or less, up to the present day.

Depictions of the hyena go back to the earliest days of human history. Approximately 32,000 years ago, Upper Palaeolithic artists daubed the impression of a cave hyena (*Crocuta crocuta spelaea*, long extinct) on the walls of what has since become known as the Chauvet Cave, in the Ardèche region of southern France. While spotted hyenas were occasionally present in the menageries of ancient Egyptian pharaohs, their main role at this time was to be fattened up for the slaughter. Hyena was apparently a regular meat at the Egyptian funerary table, and perhaps

Spotted hyena depicted on a Greek amphora.

Dogs attacking hyena, found in Deir el Medina, Egypt.

also in everyday life. A papyrus dating from the Egyptian New Kingdom, between the seventeenth and twelfth centuries BC, shows a striped hyena being savagely hunted down by three dogs.

An early reference to the hyena in Western culture is in the work of Aristotle, written between 350 and 300 BC. However, Aristotle derived his knowledge of hyenas from an earlier source – the *History of Heracles* by Herodorus – of which only a few fragments have survived. According to Aristotle, Herodorus believed the hyena mounts and is mounted in alternate years; in other words, hyenas were thought to be either hermaphrodites or sex-changers. In his *History of Animals*, Aristotle attempts to set the record straight, pointing out that Herodorus was mistaken. Yet, by trying to counter ancient rumours, Aristotle only fuelled the fire further, and – as often happens – his readers tended to remember and repeat the rumour, ignoring the attempts to refute it. Consequently, misinformation about the hyena's sex life continues to this day. Part of the problem, it seems, lies in the confusion of species. When we read Aristotle's description of the hyena in his *History of Animals*, it is clear, as hyena authority Stephen Glickman has pointed out,[2] that Aristotle and Herodorus have got their hyenas mixed up. Aristotle describes the hyena as resembling the wolf in colour, but says it is 'more shaggy, and is furnished with a mane running all along the spine'.[3] This is clearly a reference to the striped hyena, whose sexual anatomy is undistinguished, whereas Herodorus is describing the spotted hyena, whose gender and genitals can certainly seem confusing.

As often happens with titillating information, no matter how false, the notion of hyenas as hermaphrodites was too juicy to ignore. A short fable known as 'The Hyenas', generally credited to Aesop, is another source of the rumour. 'They say', writes Aesop, 'that hyenas change their sex each year and become males and females alternately. Now, one day a male hyena attempted an unnatural sex act with a female hyena. The female responded: "If you do that, friend, remember what you do to me will soon be done to you."'[4] While hardly one of Aesop's most pungent lessons, the tale is clarified by a helpful gloss from the author, who suggests that 'this is what one could

The leucrota, or crocotta, was believed to be the result of mating between a hyena and a lioness. From the *Bestiary of Anne Walsh*, c. 1400–1425.

say to the judge concerning his successor, if he had to suffer some indignity from him'.[5]

In the first century AD, the rumour was still going strong. In his *Metamorphoses*, Ovid noted that the hyena continually changes its sex and nature from male to female and back again. Pliny the Elder added further misinformation by describing the hyena (which he calls by its Latin name, *crocotta*) as a cross between a dog and a wolf. It has impossibly strong teeth, adds Pliny, and 'instant digestion', and it stands 'about the size of an ass, with a stag's haunches, a lion's neck, tail and breast, badger's head, cloven hoof, mouth opening right back to the ears, and ridges of bone in place of rows of teeth'. As an afterthought, he adds: 'only the hyena digs up graves to eat the corpses'.[6] Marcus Lucan, in his epic poem *Civil War* (AD 60–5), describes the hyena as drooling the 'foam of mad dogs' and brandishing the skin of its still-living victims, flayed alive on the battlefield.[7]

The lurid accounts continued into the third century, when Clement of Alexandria, in his *Paedagogus*, noted that the hyena is 'quite obsessed with sexual intercourse'.[8] A century later, the anonymous author of the *Physiologus* identified the hyena as the 'brute' mentioned in the Bible in Leviticus and Jeremiah. 'There is an animal which is called the hyena in Greek and the Brute in Latin', claims the *Physiologus*. 'This animal is an *arenotelicon*, that is, an alternating male–female. At one time it becomes male, at another female, and it is unclean because it has two natures.'[9]

While the hermaphrodite motif never disappeared, in medieval bestiaries it was temporarily trumped by the grave-robbing theme. In the Middle Ages, the 'Yena', as it was called (sometimes spelled 'Yenna' or 'Iena'), was usually portrayed tearing a human body from a tomb or chewing on a disinterred cadaver, and described as 'a creature that eats human corpses

Mosaic depicting a hunt, from the House of Bacchus in Djémila (Cuicul), Algeria, 5th century.

and changes sex'. Often the illustrations have a church in the background; sometimes the ground is littered with human skulls and bones. Typical of the genre is an anonymous twelfth-century Latin bestiary that, according to T. H. White's translation, refers to 'a dirty brute' called 'the YENA, which is accustomed to live in the sepulchres of the dead and devour their bodies'.[10] In the following century, the Franciscan scholar Bartholomaeus Anglicus, in his encyclopedia *On the Properties of Things*, defines the hyena as 'a cruel beast like to the wolf in devouring and gluttony, and reseth [feeds] on dead men, and taketh their carcase out of the earth, and devoureth them'.[11] Bestiaries also commonly used images of hyenas mating to warn against homosexuality, probably because of the female's bizarre genitalia. These images regularly depict slavering, dragon-like creatures with long necks and exaggerated manes, neither spotted nor striped. Like most people, no doubt, their illustrators had never laid eyes on a living hyena.

Such images, along with descriptions of the hyena's apparently supernatural qualities, led it to be regarded throughout much of history more as a legendary beast than a real creature – a monster 'without pity for the living and ominous to the dead', as it is described in a sixteenth-century Brussels tapestry.

The hyena in this illustration from a medieval bestiary looks like a grotesque dragon. Larger than a man, it has a long neck, bird-like legs and feet, a thin, feathery tail, distinctive genitals and a devilish face.

Throughout the fifteenth and sixteenth centuries, moreover, exaggerated descriptions of hyenas were commonplace in the tales of travellers returning to Europe after adventures in Africa and other exotic parts. Most notable of these was the author known as Leo Africanus, a Moor who converted to Christianity, whose *History and Description of Africa* was written in Arabic *circa* 1526 and translated into English in 1600. Despite his travels to places where hyenas were common, Leo Africanus spins a fanciful tale, describing the hyena as resembling a wolf in size and shape, 'saving that his legges and feete are like to the legs and feete of a man'. He repeats the rumour that hyenas 'will rake the carkeises of men out of their graves, and will devour them', concluding with an account of how this 'abject and silly creature' is seduced out of his cave by drums and music so he can be tied up and killed.[12]

In this detail from a bestiary, the hyena is shown standing on its hind legs, munching hungrily on the torso of a human corpse.

In 1551 the Swiss naturalist Conrad Gesner wrote a careful and fully illustrated natural history – translated, revised, compressed and extended by the English cleric and author Edward Topsell – which was one of the first such texts to distinguish between different kinds of hyenas. 'The first and vulgar kind of Hyaena is bred in Affricke and Arabia', wrote Topsell, 'being in quantity of body like a wolfe, but much rougher haird, for it hath bristles like a horsses mane all along his back'.[13] So far, so good – this is a concise and accurate description of the striped hyena. Topsell continues, however, noting that 'the middle of his backe is a little crooked or dented, the colour yellowish, but bespeckled on the sides with blew spots, which make him looke more terrible, as if it had so many eies'.[14] The drawing that accompanies the text looks more like a spotted than a striped hyena; however, to confuse matters further, the spots on the creature's pelt are made up of parallel stripes.

This hyena looks more like a lioness with a dorsal mane. Her genitals are distinctly female, and she sports an attractive red sash.

In the seventeenth century Sir Thomas Browne, in his *Pseudodoxia Epidemica*, dismissed rumours about the hyena's hermaphroditism and annual changing of sex, since this would transgress the natural 'Laws of their Coition', which only man has been so bold and venal as to break.[15] In his *History of the World* (1614), Sir Walter Raleigh, discussing Noah's Ark, explains that, since there would not have been enough room for every animal, it would not have been necessary to take animals that were offshoots of other species, such as the hyena, which Raleigh describes as the 'offspring' of 'Foxes and Wolves'.[16]

This fearful animal's monstrous reputation was compounded when, between 1764 and 1767, an obscure, hyena-like beast terrorized the region of Gévaudan in southeast France. The story of

'Hyena', from Manuel Philes, *De animalium proprietate*, c. 1533.

this creature is tangled and complicated, and the different witness reports continue to baffle historians and cryptozoologists to this day, but it is widely accepted that the Beast of Gévaudan killed over a hundred victims over three years, many of them children, by tearing out their throats with its teeth. The beast – or beasts, as some eyewitness reports mention two creatures – was supposedly the size of a large calf with a big, brown, wolf-like head and a body covered in reddish fur. Its ears were straight, its chest white and broad, and it was always described as agile and

'The Second Kind of Hyaena', from Edward Topsell, *Historie of Foore-Footed Beastes* (1658).

'Spotted hyena Devouring its Prey', from Johann Johnston, *Historia Naturalis: De Quadrupedibus* (1650).

'Spotted Hyena', from Olfert Dapper, *Description of Africa* (1668).

strong, and often sighted in two distant locations on the same day. These are the points on which most accounts agree.

Other reports diverge. Some witnesses recall a strong odour; others observed no odour at all. Some mentioned a long, thick tail with a white tip. Some claimed the back legs ended in horse-like hooves, whereas the front legs were shorter, covered with long fur, and with six claws to each paw. One witness claims to have seen the beast crossing a river by raising itself on its hind legs and wading across like a human being; a shepherd reports observing it standing up on its rear legs and lifting a fully grown sheep. Some described it as crawling along with its belly to the ground; others claim it could make huge leaps when running. The creature was finally shot and killed by a local farmer and innkeeper named Jean Chastel.[17]

The provenance and identity of this frightening creature have never been fully resolved; the most prosaic explanation is that it was an oversized wolf. However, it has been ascertained

Captain William Cornwallis Harris, 'Spotted hyenas, "fuscous" brown hyenas and African Wild Dogs', from *Portraits of the Game and Wild Animals of Southern Africa* (1840).

that Chastel's son Antoine kept a striped hyena in his menagerie, and a taxidermist at the National Museum of Natural History in Paris later discovered that a stuffed specimen similar to the creature shot by Jean Chastel had been kept in the collection from 1766 until 1819. When the creature in the museum was successfully identified as a striped hyena, it was suggested that the Chastels may have created the story of the Beast of Gévaudan in order to cover up the fact that one of them was either a serial killer or accustomed to taking his hyena on killing sprees in the local forests. However unlikely this may seem, there is historical evidence for the use of trained hyenas in hunting. In 1790 the Scottish traveller James Bruce observed that, in the Cape of South Africa, the spotted hyena was sometimes domesticated in the houses of the peasantry, among whom 'he is preferred to the dog himself for attachment to his master, for general sagacity, and even, it is said, for his qualifications for the chase'.[18] In 1801 Sir John Barrow, in *An Account of Travels into the Interior of Southern Africa*, described how spotted hyenas in the Snow Mountains in South Africa were trained to hunt game, writing that they were 'as faithful and diligent as any of the common domestic dogs'.[19]

Swedish naturalist Anders Sparrman, in a 1789 account of his travels in South Africa, repeats the usual story about the hyena being a cruel and formidable beast living by depredation and rapine. James Bruce, in 1790, paints an equally harrowing picture of troops of hyenas following in the wake of the Hottentot and Caffre armies, ravaging hastily made graves and gorging on the corpses of the slain. 'In a word, the hyaena was the plague of our lives, the terror of our night-walks', he remarks, after describing how he was woken from his bed one night to confront 'large blue eyes glaring at me in the dark'. A hyena had slipped into his tent and was 'standing nigh the head of the bed, with two or three large bunches of candles in his mouth'. The beast did not seem threatening, and 'as his mouth was full, and he had no claws to tear with, I was not afraid of him', yet to be on the safe side, Bruce stabbed the creature 'as near the heart as I could judge' with his pike, while his servant 'cleft his skull with a battle-axe'.[20] With hyenas, it seems, you can never be too careful.

HYENAS IN THE MODERN AGE

Before the eighteenth century, such accounts were all most people had to go on, since very few would ever have lain eyes on a hyena outside picture books or natural histories. During the

'Spotted and
Striped Hyenas',
from Comte de
Buffon, *Histoire
Naturelle* (1830).
Note the scattered
bones and skulls.

late eighteenth and early nineteenth centuries, however, hyenas
were occasionally to be found in menageries, zoos, circuses and
travelling fairs. In Britain, Bostock and Wombwell's travelling
menagerie (1805–1917) had two spotted hyenas and one striped
hyena, which it eventually handed over to Whipsnade Zoo in
Bedfordshire, and a broadside announcing the menagerie of
Hermann von Aken in Hanover, dated 23 November 1830,
depicts a man holding open the jaws of a spotted hyena.

According to historical records, an Italian gentleman by the name of Stephen Polito owned a menagerie that toured around England in the late eighteenth century. Polito went into partnership with a menagerist named Miles in 1798, and Miles and Polito's Menagerie, which boasted among its exhibits a 'laughing hyena', exhibited at St Bartholomew's Fair in 1799 and Nottingham Goose Fair in 1807. Polito acquired a permanent menagerie from the Pidcock family in 1810, and continuing to tour in the summer, exhibited his animals at Exeter Exchange on the Strand, London, in the winter. Polito's brother John acquired the collection after Stephen's death; John's father-in-law Edward Cross was the next owner, at which point it became known as Cross's Menagerie. This small zoo, according to visitors, was full of cages and enclosures, all far too small and smelly by modern standards, and even included an elephant, which had to be destroyed in 1826 when it tried to break out of its pen (its skeleton was subsequently exhibited in the same enclosure).

For a while, Cross's Menagerie was extremely popular. Notable figures such as William Wordsworth and Lord Byron

Jean-Baptiste Oudry, *Hyena Attacked by Two Dogs*, 1739, oil on canvas.

THE TORTOISE SHELL HYÆNA, OR HYÆNA DOG.

In the Gardens of the Zoological Society.

An African wild dog, which is mislabelled here as a 'Tortoise Shell Hyaena, or Hyaena Dog in the Gardens of the Zoological Society', from Comte de Buffon's *Histoire Naturelle* (1834).

visited the zoo; artists like Edwin Landseer and Jacques-Laurent Agasse painted its animals, and the collection was represented on pearlware pottery. In 1822 the geologist William Buckland was able to determine that Kirkdale Cave in North Yorkshire was once used as a hyena den; he did so by comparing the gnawed bones from the cave to the bones given to the laughing hyena in Cross's Menagerie, which closed not long after the opening of the Zoological Gardens in Regent's Park in 1828. The nineteenth-century Londoner interested in hyenas might also have visited the menagerie at the Tower of London, which contained a spotted hyena notable for managing (with no apparent effort) to tear up a two-and-a-half-metre-long plank nailed to the floor of its recently repaired enclosure.

In the eighteenth and nineteenth centuries information about hyenas contained in books of natural history was a little

Friedrich Specht, *Striped Hyena*, from J. G. Wood, *Animate Creation* (1885).

more accurate in terms of their physical characteristics, though not in terms of their essential nature. In 1830 the Comte de Buffon, in his *Natural History of Quadrupeds*, describes the hyena as 'extremely ferocious', and in *The Romance of Natural History*, published in 1863, the very thought of this horrible beast leads author Philip Henry Gosse on a flight of lyrical fancy:

You hear . . . amidst the deep roar rises from the gaunt heaps of stone an unearthly sound, like the laugh of a demon. Again, the cackling mirth echoes along the ruined halls, as if exulting in the wild war of the elements, and in the desolation around. Lo! from out of yon low arch, in the Place of Tombs, gleam two fiery eyes, and forth stalks into the lightning the fell hyena. With bristling mane and grinning teeth, the obscene monster glares at you, and warns you to secure a timely retreat. Another appears, bearing in its jaws a loathsome human skull, which it has found in the caravan track. You shudder as you hear the bones crack and grind between the powerful teeth, and gladly shrink away from the repulsive vicinity.[21]

If this description seems vivid, it is subtle in comparison to that published in a children's natural history book of 1860. 'Their form is ungraceful and disagreeable', remarks the anonymous author in his discussion of the spotted hyena, 'with a large truncated head set on a protruded and stiff neck, high fore-legs, a short body, and low hind quarters, a long bristly mane, ranging from the nape of the neck to the tail, a wallowing gait, great personal uncleanliness and a horrible voice – no beast of the forest or plain offers a more disgusting aspect'. And this is before we get to 'the offensive odours of their carrion breath' and 'the disagreeable smell of their body'.[22]

Less purple but equally off the mark is naturalist J. F. Nott, who states in his book of 1886, *Wild Animals: Photographed and Described*: 'All writers agree that the hyaena lacks courage, and is only ferocious when he himself is free from harm.' He relates an incident involving a 'well known Indian sportsman' who found himself face-to-face with a hyena. Although he had previously not 'wished to waste a shot', now, thinks the sportsman, 'although I had spared it before, I could not resist taking his worthless life as he stood'.[23] And in their *Introduction to the Study of Mammals* (1891), Flower and Lydekker characterize the striped hyena as 'essentially a cowardly animal', though they distinguish it from the spotted variety, which, they claim, is 'larger and bolder . . . hunting in packs, and uttering very frequently its unearthly cry'.[24] In his *Natural History* (1893–4), Richard Lydekker adds that 'the striped hyaena – probably on account of its body-snatching propensities – is cordially detested by the natives of all the countries it inhabits'. He continues: 'when a hyaena is killed, the body is treated in many parts of India with every mark of indignity, and finally burnt'.[25]

The Victorian period was the great age of natural histories, all of which perpetuated the reputation of hyenas as cowardly

Gustav Mützel, 'Brown Hyena', from Richard Lydekker, *The Royal Natural History*, vol. III (1895).

and malign. A brief survey of nineteenth-century texts produces the following comments. Hyenas, we are told (and there is usually no distinction made between the different species), are 'repulsive looking', 'a most mysterious and awful animal', 'rank and coarse', 'singularly coarse and ferocious in character', with 'revolting habits', 'adapted to gorge on the grossest animal substances, dead or alive, fresh or corrupted'. They are 'the scavengers of the desert, feeding on dead carcasses', 'always to be found roaming about burial grounds and digging out the dead', and 'cordially detested by the natives of all the countries it inhabits'. All in all, the hyena 'is a gloomy, ill-looking animal; and its manners and habits correspond with its appearance'.

The nineteenth-century media regularly presented hyenas as dangerous (though cowardly) beasts prone to escape from menageries and bite the hands that fed them. Often, such hyperbolic accounts conclude with reports of the hyena finding its way to the nearest cemetery and proceeding to dig up dead bodies. In

Striped hyenas with skeletons.

A. Fournier, a jackal and a rather sheepish-looking striped hyena, engraving from Charles d'Orbigny and E. Martinet, *Dictionnaire universel d'histoire naturelle* (1873).

these semi-mythical stories, no distinction is ever made between different types of hyena, and the errant beasts are invariably gunned down by some local hero, often a brave police chief, football player or fire fighter. For example, in western Ohio, in February 1858, a 'very ferocious' hyena escaped from a menagerie and the next day followed its 'terrible instincts' and 'was discovered in the graveyard, having dug up and partly devoured two or three dead bodies'. When a mob of citizens cornered 'the monster', it 'turned on its assailants', crushing the head of one man in its jaws and 'killing him instantly', and 'tearing the flesh from the right arm and chest of a lad who is not expected to recover'.[26]

In 1910 a hyena escaped from Bostock's Animal Show at New York's Coney Island and was shot down in front of the West Eighth Street Police Station; 'the body was found to have received forty-one bullet wounds'.[27] (Bostock's hyenas seem to have given him a lot of trouble; four years earlier, he was sued for $15,000 when one of his hyenas bit off one half of the index finger of a woman's left hand.[28]) A hyena broke out of its cage on a British steamship in April 1894 'to the terror and danger of all on board'. When the crew attempted to catch it, this 'dangerous brute' retreated to a corner, 'snarling and showing his teeth'. The animal was eventually caught in ropes and 'dragged into his cage, amid the loud cheers of his amateur hunters'.[29] And a 'vicious hyena' named Jim caused something of a stir in the summer of 1897 when he escaped from Chicago's Lincoln Park Zoo by gnawing a hole in the door of his cage. Three days later, he was spotted at night in Sheridan Park 'skulking' along the roadway, holding his snout high in the air and sniffing. The fugitive hyena ended up in Graceland Cemetery, 'where with unerring instinct he had made his way immediately after his escape [and had] made night hideous with his howls'. The

following day, Jim was located 'ravaging graves' in the cemetery. He 'terrorized the city' for six days, until he was shot on the morning of 22 June.[30]

Well into the twentieth century, otherwise sedate, objective sources of information are unable to refrain from a sneering tone when called upon to describe the hyena. In E. P. Walker's authoritative *Mammals of the World* (1968), the author asserts, wrongly, that 'spotted hyenas are cowardly and will not fight if their prospective victim defends itself'.[31] And as late as 1976, the fifteenth edition of the *Encyclopædia Britannica* refers to the 'cowardice' of the striped hyena. Moreover, the tradition of inaccurate illustrations continued well into the modern era, when, on stamps and postcards and in picture books, all kinds of creatures were blithely labelled 'hyenas'. A stamp from Mauritius depicts a 'striped hyena' that looks more like a sloth. Striped hyenas are regularly labelled as spotted, and vice versa.

Gustav Mützel, 'The Striped and Spotted Hyaenas in the Gardens of the Zoological Society', from Richard Lydekker, *The Royal Natural History* (1893–4).

Striped and spotted hyena stamps, Mauritius. The striped hyena looks more like a sloth.

opposite: 'Painted Hyena', lithograph, 1840.

When they are not slavering monsters, they resemble badgers or wombats. More often, they are confused with jackals and African wild dogs, both of which are smaller in size than hyenas; moreover, jackals have fox-like snouts and African wild dogs are variegated in colour, with large, rounded ears.

Schöngezeichnete Hyäne. Hyæna picta.
Hyène peinte.

3 Hyena Magic

The hyena is depicted in African folklore as an abnormal and ambivalent animal: considered to be sly, brutish, necrophagous, dangerous, and the vilest of beasts.
Jürgen Frembgen, *The Magicality of the Hyena*, 1998

The annals of natural history, explored in the previous chapter, show that the hyena has long been characterized as one of the untouchables of the animal world. In its mythological and magical roles, too, this unusual beast is widely reviled as a grotesque, hideous scavenger that battens on decay. In every unhallowed realm, whether graveyard or battlefield, hyenas are rumoured to be skulking, raising loathsome prospects and – according to reputation – excremental smells. Observing the number of beasts that feature in cultural mythologies, anthropologists from J. G. Frazer onwards have pointed out that animals are vehicles for embodying emotionally charged ideas. Foolishly, we humans tend to conflate ugliness with evil, and since we find the hyena viscerally repulsive, we class it with 'every creeping thing that creepeth upon the earth', all condemned by Leviticus as 'abominations' (11:41). But watch out. As Freud suggests, whatever we repress will come back to bite us – and the hyena's jaws are built to crush bone.

Most people are not aware that the female spotted hyena has unusually formed genitals, and do not automatically consider hyenas to be anatomical pariahs; still, rumours about hyena hermaphrodites have never completely disappeared. Interestingly, however, these myths have crossed over from the spotted hyena to her striped and brown cousins, which, in folklore, are

Johann Christian Daniel Schreber, 'Spotted Hyena', copperplate engraving from *Die Säugthiere in Abbildungen nach der Natur mit Beschreibungen* (1775).

Hyaenas Contending over the Body of an Ass, 1895, wood-engraving.

also associated with gender-bending and weird sex magic. Even anthropologists rarely differentiate between spotted and striped hyenas when both species inhabit the same territory, and in many local languages both types go by the same name. Some have speculated that stories about the African spotted hyena – orally transmitted by traders, nomads and migrants – travelled north and east from Ethiopia, for example, to western and southern Asia, where they were applied to the local (striped) hyena population. Another possibility is that spotted hyenas were once common in Asia, and although they are no longer found there, traditional beliefs remain, and have been transferred by later generations onto striped hyenas. Either way, no species of hyena has escaped denigration.

SEX MAGIC

According to anthropologists, the ritual value of animals is deeply connected to the taboos and fetishes we have developed around them, which, in turn, affect whether or not we make use of their bodies. The hyena's body, shrouded in taboo, has been the source of fetish objects ever since the ancient Greeks and Romans used its blood, excrement, rectum, genitalia, eyes, tongue, hair, skin and fat to make charms that both averted evil and promised fertility. In the ancient world, it was believed that the genitalia of a hyena would hold a couple peaceably together and that a hyena anus worn as an amulet on the upper arm would make its male possessor irresistible to women.

Karl Joseph Brodtmann, 'Spotted and Striped Hyenas', lithograph from Heinrich Schinz, *Natural History and Images of Man and Mammals* (1840).

Karl Joseph Brodtmann, 'Spotted and Striped Hyenas', from Heinrich Schinz, *Natural History and Images of Man and Mammals* (1840).

Gefleckte Hyäne   Hyæna crocuta.   La Hyène tachetée.

1/7

Gestreifte Hyäne.   Hyæna striata.   La Hyène rayée.

1/9

In his *History of Animals*, Aristotle notes that in making fetishes and spells, 'the Magi have held in the highest admiration the hyaena of all animals',[1] and goes on to list the qualities of charms and totems made from the body of this unusually potent beast. Similarly, Pliny observes: 'barrenness in women is cured by a [hyena] eye taken in food with liquorice and dill, conception being guaranteed in three days'.[2] He also points out that 'a hyaena's genitals taken in honey stimulate desire . . . even when men hate intercourse with women', since 'the peace of the whole household is assured by keeping in the home these genitals and a vertebra with the hide still adhering to them'.[3]

Today, in Afghanistan, India and many parts of Asia, striped hyenas – although widely feared – are nevertheless associated with fertility, and their body parts play an important role in sex magic. The thick hair of the mane and tail is especially long and elastic, and the association of such hair with female beauty has made it an important component of love charms (while the animal itself, ironically, is considered hideous). The striped hyena's blood is used in folk medicine, and its tongue is supposed to fight tumours. In the Pakistani province of Sindh, the local Muslims place the tooth of a striped hyena over their churns in order not to lose the milk's blessing, and the Bedouin of Arabia use striped hyena meat as medicine. In Iranian folklore, a dried hyena pelt is considered a potent charm to change the heart of a reluctant lover, and in the Khyber area, burned hyena fat is applied to a man's genitals or sometimes taken orally to ensure virility.

Among the people of western Sudan, the possession of a striped hyena's nose is a magical way to guarantee a good harvest, and a tail will help get you the woman of your choice. In Afghanistan, the vulva (*kus*) of a female striped hyena is believed to have aphrodisiac powers, and some mullahs will wear a hyena *kus* wrapped in silk under their armpits for a week. Among the

Pakhtun, the *kus* is kept in vermilion powders, and if a man wants to win the object of his desire, he is supposed to peer at her through this now-scarlet *kus*, made into a sort of monocle; this is apparently the source of a Dari expression: 'it will happen as smoothly as if you'd looked through a striped hyena's vulva'. In a similar display of sympathetic magic, homosexuals and bisexuals are said to attract young men by means of a freshly killed striped hyena's penis or rectum (if possible, cut out of a freshly dead animal while the anal sphincter is still twitching), giving rise to the Pashto phrase for someone who attracts many lovers: 'He has the anus of a striped hyena.'

The Himba people of Namibia, who live closely with spotted hyenas, believe the phallic shape of hyena genitalia indicates they are all males and therefore homosexual. They are characterized in Himba folklore as *omayova*, a word meaning 'acting contrary to normal behaviour', 'repellent', 'stigmatized' and 'set apart'. Anthropologist D. P. Crandall, a specialist on the Himba, explains that this is because the hyena's presumed physiological abnormality is 'compounded with a moral classification that creates a strong correspondence between the homosexual and the hyena'. Homosexuality, Crandall adds, is 'almost unfathomable' among the Himba, though there are often rumours of homosexuals living in far-off villages or distant towns.[4] According to anthropologist Alma Gottleib, the West African Beng believe that if you happen to find a dead spotted hyena with its rectum still moving in and out, you must immediately plug and quieten the anus; otherwise, you may be struck by the curse of perpetual laughter, which is a sure sign of your impending death.[5] Gottleib's informant told her the following story:

> One day, perhaps about a century ago, a hyena had come
> in from the forest and defecated on the ground, causing

the entire village to be *wi*, 'broken': had the village not been evacuated . . . it would soon have been the locus of innumerable deaths. Thus, the villagers immediately abandoned the old village and chose the present site.[6]

Gustav Mützel, 'A Gathering of Striped Hyenas', from Richard Lydekker, *The Royal Natural History* (1893–4).

BLACK MAGIC

The hyena has long been associated with necromancy and with evil spirits, no doubt because, as Aristotle claims, 'it is exceedingly fond of putrefied flesh, and will burrow in a graveyard to gratify this propensity'.[7] True, the hyena's tendency to scavenge for food means that it often lives in the proximity of death and dead bodies, though these are rarely human ones, except those on battlefields. Nevertheless, its scavenging tendencies, nocturnal

Alfred Kubin,
a striped hyena
on the battlefield,
illustration from
the Czech periodical
Zeit-Echo (1915),
lithograph on
laid paper.

habits and uncanny ability to chew and absorb bone are all probably the source of folklore concerning the hyena's dark magic. Aristotle, in 'On Marvellous Things Heard', says of the hyena that 'when it sees some wild beast, before itself being seen, or steps on the shadow of a man, produces speechlessness, and fixes them to the spot in such a way that they cannot move their body; and it is said that they do this in the case of dogs also'.[8] According to J. G. Frazer, 'the ancients supposed that in Arabia, if a hyaena trod on a man's shadow, it deprived him of the power of speech and motion; and that if a dog, standing on a roof in the moonlight, cast a shadow on the ground and a hyaena trod on it, the dog would fall down as if dragged with a rope'.[9]

Aristotle also advanced the notion that the hyena's neck consisted of one single, jointless bone, and according to the author of the article in *Harper's New Monthly Magazine* (1854), this is an assertion 'which, it is almost needless to add, is to the full as groundless as that this peculiar bone proved of great efficacy in magical invocation; which belief is to this day current among the superstitious Arabs, who, when they slay one of these animals, carefully bury the head, lest it should operate as an avenging charm or spell'.[10]

Other long-standing hyena lore includes the rumour that any beast looked at three times by a hyena will be unable to move, and the myth that the hyena can hypnotize both men and animals with the touch of its left paw. Some say that the hyena's appetite for carrion is so huge that it will empty itself forcibly by squeezing between two trees before going back for seconds. More menacingly, the hyena is widely believed to have the power to cast its spirits into others (including humans), causing them to become possessed. Among the Bedouin, even today, according to anthropologist Dan Boneh, there is a widespread belief in the hyena's power to lure away anyone walking alone at night (like the vampire, the hyena becomes powerful only after the sun has gone down). When 'hit with the vapours of the hyena's anal-gland scent', according to Bedouin folklore, 'the person will no longer be able to exercise conscious judgements' and, spellbound, 'follows the animal's path as if enslaved'. In such tales, Boneh reports, the hyena's victims are hypnotized into believing the hyena is their master. 'One Bedouin reported an incident in which a relative who failed to appear at a scheduled time was found in a nearby valley with his head inside a hyena's cave, desperately trying to enter.'[11]

Folklore is full of such dark spirits, and our fear of them is not so much the fear of bodily injury as the fear of things happening within our own bodies and minds over which we have no control. Many people, even those who have never seen one, admit to a certain uncanny feeling about the hyena, as though

it were invested with some kind of supernatural power. Freud, in his essay on the Uncanny, describes this feeling as a very particular sensation of dread and horror. 'The German word "*unheimlich*"', he explains, 'is obviously the opposite of "*heimlich*" ["homely"] . . . the opposite of what is familiar; and we are tempted to conclude that what is "uncanny" is frightening precisely because it is *not* known and familiar'.[12] Animals that are tame and companionable to man, Freud points out, are considered *heimlich*, but not all wild animals are *unheimlich*; only certain frightening creatures, of which the hyena is perhaps the most unmistakable.

In the final section of his essay, Freud reveals that the uncanny is, in fact, something that is secretly familiar, something that has undergone repression and then returned from it. In other words, the *heimlich* becomes a secret form of the *unheimlich* at the point at which things are brought to light. With this in mind, the uncanny nature of the hyena appears to be closely connected to its habit of unearthing dead bodies from graves and

'Witch Human Beings Turn To Animals', poster from Ghana published in *Fortean Times* (August 2009).

'The Hyena', 1842.

feeding on carrion. If premature burial is a supremely uncanny phenomenon, then so is premature *unburial*, the bringing to light of the dead body, which is normally hidden from consciousness and, like death in general, is rightfully repressed.

The idea of the uncanny is closely related to the concept of animism, discussed at length by J. G. Frazer. In *Totem and Taboo*, a work closely influenced by Frazer's *The Golden Bough* (1890), Freud explains how 'the assumptions of magic are more fundamental and older than the doctrine of spirits, which forms the kernel of animism'.[13] Magic, he explains, is 'the technique of animism' that 'reveals in the clearest and most unmistakable way an intention to impose the laws governing mental life upon real things'.[14] This principle is clearly at work in the belief that the qualities of the hyena may be shared with anyone who possesses part of its invulnerable body. In his *History of Animals*, Aristotle informs us that people carrying items made of hyena leather will not be attacked; the skin of a hyena head can cure headaches; the hyena's teeth will cure toothache when touched to the corresponding human tooth; and the hyena's gall, when applied to the forehead, cures ophthalmia.

In the dark, especially when reflected by the light of the moon or fire, the hyena's eyes appear to flash red; if angry, they can seem black and opaque. These optical anomalies are no doubt the source of legends regarding the 'hyena stone' mentioned by Pliny and repeated in various medieval bestiaries, as well as in Iranian folklore. According to legend, this shining, many-coloured talisman is found in the hyena's eye, and when placed under the tongue will reveal the future.

In parts of Africa, the hyena is the equivalent of our black cat – the witch's familiar. To heighten their status in the community, witch-doctors in Tanzania have been known to steal spotted hyena cubs from their den while the mother is away. In

Capischos   Schnarrthier
Ryzaena   capensis
Le   Suricate   du Cap
2/3

Lalandische   Zibethgiane
Proteles   Lalandii
Le   Proteles
2/6

J. J. Honnegger, 'A Striped Hyena and his Distant Relation, the Meerkat', from Heinrich Schinz, *Natural History and Images of Man and Mammals* (1840).

Tanzania, as in northern India, witches are said to travel through the night on the backs of flying hyenas, carrying gourds of hyena butter as torch fuel. In many African cultures, hyenas are associated with witchcraft and divination; their hearts and livers may be vital ingredients in magic spells. In southern Senegal, among the Kujamaat Diola people, hyenas are considered to be the close kin of lepers. Like the homosexual or hermaphrodite, the leper is regarded as a marginal figure generally symbolizing immorality, dirty habits, the reversal of normal activities and other negative traits. If a Kujamaat hunter kills a hyena, he must carry the carcass with respect, to prevent the animal's malevolent spirit from taking revenge.

Hyena amulet from Egypt, Ptolemaic Dynasty, 664–30 BC, ivory.

As folklorist William Bascom explains in his work on West African Yoruba proverbs, sometimes Hyena is a trickster, but more often he is the gull of his smarter acquaintance, Hare.[15] According to one story, during a famine in the bush, Hyena and Hare decide to sell their mothers to buy millet. Hyena ties his mother up with a solid cord but the clever Hare uses a fragile rope, allowing his mother to break free and escape. Hare pretends to be very sorry, and the two creatures sell Hyena's mother instead, and share the millet. Unless Hyena has ulterior motives (hyena mothers, remember, are notoriously tough), superior intelligence is not a feature of the hyena's mythic counterpart.

In pre-Islamic Arabic poetry, female hyenas are seen indulging in a wide range of transgressive behaviours, including eating those toward whom we usually recognize social obligations (their hosts, for example, or fallen enemies), as well as the sexual exploitation of fallen warriors. The fourteenth-century Arab author al-Nuwayri writes in his encyclopedic *Nihayat al-Arab*:

J. J. Honnegger, Striped hyena and unrelated African wild dog, from Heinrich Schinz, *Natural History and Images of Man and Mammals* (1840).

the female hyena has a passion for digging up graves, and this is solely because of her craving for human flesh. It is her habit, when a slain man is left in a deserted place and the corpse has swollen and the penis is engorged, to come up to it, then mount it and gratify her needs on it. Then she eats it.[16]

Fig. 42.

Fig. 43.

According to scholar Suzanne Stetkevych, the female hyena's supposed feasting and fertility in the face of death – laughing with delight – forms a direct contrast to the female human tradition of mourning, wailing and abstinence. The Arabic verb meaning 'to laugh' is the same as the verb meaning 'to menstruate', which suggests this double entendre may be at the root of pre-Islamic depictions of female hyenas as queens of disruption and degradation, rulers of the realm of waste. In some Arab cultures, both male and female hyenas were believed to menstruate, thereby breaching the boundaries of nature.[17] Calling everything into question, the hyena, mistress of mayhem, disrupts our attempts at order, threatening and distorting our neat vision of the everyday world.

Crucial to the hyena's shady reputation are the characteristic sounds made by the spotted variety – sounds that we in the West describe as 'laughter', which, however, is only one interpretation of their sinister resonance. Aristotle, wide of the mark again, believed that the hyena made 'a noise that resembles the retching noise of a man vomiting' to lure dogs within its reach (such dogs being unable, presumably, to resist the lure of human vomit). In other times and places, however, the hyena's vocalizations have been seen as attempts at human speech. 'These hideous brutes', says Pliny in his *Natural History*, 'are wont to repair to the shepherds' huts and imitate the human voice, and even learn some person's name, who, when he answers to the call and comes out, is immediately torn to pieces.'[18] This fallacy has its roots in a passage in Aelian's *On the Characteristics of Animals*, from the second century AD, in which the hyena is referred to as a *korokotta*. Says the author:

I shall now relate the villainy of the Korokottai, of which I have actually heard. It conceals itself in thickets and then listens to woodcutters calling one another by name, and even to anything they say. And then it imitates their voices and speaks (though the story may be fabulous) with a voice that sounds human at any rate, calling out the name which it has heard. And the man who has been called approaches: the animal withdraws and calls again: the man follows the voice all the more. But when it has drawn him away from his fellow-workers and has got him alone, it seizes him and kills him and then makes a meal of him after luring him on with its call.[19]

HYENA MEN

Along with its eerie vocalizations, the social aspects of the spotted hyena's behaviour mark out this haunting animal as a candidate for shape shifting. A nocturnal scavenger feeding on the dead, the hyena inhabits the liminal zone between human and non-human, a time and place where occult forces prevail. According to Greek lore, ghostly hyenas will sometimes haunt battlefields, where they drink the blood of dying soldiers. In the Near and Middle East, striped hyenas are generally regarded as physical incarnations of jinns. The Persian physician and cosmographer Zakariya al-Qazwini, in his thirteenth-century treatise 'Marvels of Creatures and Strange Things Existing', refers to a tribe called the 'hyena people', and informs us that, should one of this tribe be in a group of a thousand men, a hyena would be able to pick him out to eat. A Persian medical treatise written around the same time warns of a hybrid man-hyena, similar to a werewolf, that attacks people in the dark.

In many societies today – in Ethiopia, Nigeria and the Sudan, for example – the form of the hyena is considered mutable. At certain times and places, humans may become hyenas, and

Hyena mask,
Mali, 20th century,
wood.

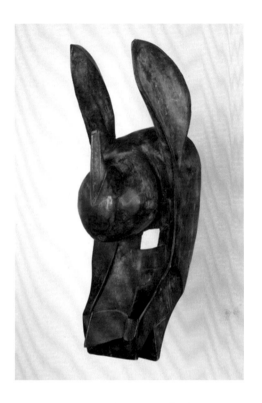

hyenas human. When considering such folklore, it is important
to bear in mind that in many tribal cultures, the state of being
human is widely regarded as part of a series of transitions, one
of many possible states of existence that are not limited by birth
and death. Humans with animal features are also known to be
common images and icons in cultures that are going through
the transition from hunter-gatherer societies to agricultural
ones. Many of the gods and goddesses of ancient Egypt, for
example, have a human torso and the head of a beast, whether
crocodile, ibis, jackal, falcon or cat. In western Sudan, people

tell legends of half-man, half-hyena man-eaters who shape-shift in the middle of the night and are reputed, like similar Western bogeymen, to prey on petting lovers. In their human form, these creatures often have a tell-tale hairy body and gleaming eyes. Similar figures appear frequently in African folklore. Anthropologist Allen F. Roberts, in his book *Animals in African Art*, reproduces photographs of hyena masks that are commonly worn by dancers in a number of African cultures. Roberts observes that 'people can "become" hyenas to play dramatic roles that usually run counter to social harmony or the tenets of human civilization'.[20] In the guise of a hyena, ordinarily civilized

Hyena mask, made by the Winiama people, Burkina Faso, c. 19th century, wood and pigment.

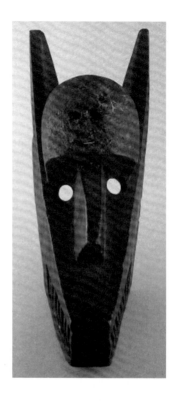

Hyena mask, made by the Bamana people, Mali, c. 19th century, wood, cowrie shells and pigment.

people can indulge in dirty tricks and nasty habits, evoking fear and disgust among the observers, who are thereby encouraged to avoid such habits in their own lives. In Sudan, such 'hyena men' are reputed to live on the fringes of villages or in the space between two villages, where they can keep a lookout in two directions at once. In the stories that are told about them, these hyena men are regularly defeated by either a man whose fiancée lives in one of the villages or a man with fiancées in both villages. The point of these stories, it seems, is to distinguish two different kinds of alliances – the demonic, illegitimate alliance of man and hyena versus the consensual alliance of legal relations.

Ethiopian Christians consider the Jews in their midst as *buda* – hyena people who cross the line between the human and the non-human.[21] Sometimes, moreover, different kinds of hyena men can be seen in the flesh. In April 2004 a BBC news report revealed that a shepherd living in the small town of Qabri Bayah, in eastern Ethiopia, had trained a male spotted hyena named Ali for use as a livestock guardian dog. 'When the Hyena feels the urge to mate, then there is the danger of it leaving in search of a female one. But I have already considered this and I now put certain herbs in its food to reduce its sexual urge', said the shepherd, I Seyyid Abdiweli Abdishakur. He apparently learned the secret from his late father, who, he says, was know-ledgeable about many things.[22]

Hyenas have been part of Ethiopian tradition for many years. In *Notes from the Hyena's Belly* (2000), a memoir of grow-ing up in Jijiga during the fall of Emperor Selassie, author Nega Mezlekia recalls being told folktales in which Hyena ended up as the dupe. He also recalls childhood games involving the hyenas that lurked on the edges of town, such as chasing them and getting as close as possible to the pack without blinking. Other games included throwing stones at hyenas, taunting them and encouraging them to enter the city at night, to clean up the rubbish in the streets.

Spotted hyenas are commonplace in the Ethiopian town of Harar, especially in the old town district, where they can be seen after nightfall walking down the narrow streets and emerging from drainage holes. The townspeople tolerate and even feel affection for these semi-urbanized hyenas, which lurk all night long on the soccer fields, coming closer to the city walls at dusk to be fed. According to legends told to tourists, this tradition began after the great famine of the late nineteenth century, and it has continued so that in times of drought or hunger the hyenas will remain on good terms with the citizens and will not maraud the city. However, the tradition of hyena feeding at the walls actually began in the 1950s. There is an older tradition of feeding porridge to hyenas, but this takes place at shrines away from Harar.

The current hyena man of Harar is Yusuf Mumee Saleh, who feeds the hyenas at the shrine of Aw Ansar. Better known, however, is a man named Mulugeta Wolde Mariam, who took over from the last hyena feeder at Assumberi. Mulugeta's nightly ritual has become a popular spectacle for tourists and sightseers. Every evening at dusk, with only his car headlights for illumination, Mulugeta calls to the spotted hyenas that live just outside the city walls, allegedly recognizing each animal by name as their luminous eyes begin appearing in the dusk. Mulugeta employs three men: one to feed the hyenas, one to collect money and one to stock baskets of meat. He claims to know the animals individually, and speaks to them in 'hyena language'.

Those familiar with local tradition, however, say that the names are made up on the spot, and are different every time. They also say that Mulugeta's men throw rocks at the hyenas to prevent them from passing by the walled section of the road and entering the town until nine o'clock each evening, at which point, when enough tourists have gathered, they dump meat outside the city walls, and the hyenas are free to pass and go into the old town. For a fee of $5, Mulugeta will let tourists feed the hyenas, even – if they are brave enough – letting them hold a skewer in their mouths from which the hyenas take pieces of raw meat. Despite losing a finger, Mulugeta denies that his job is dangerous. While he has spoken of his plan to pass on his secrets to others so that the tradition will not die out, locals

Hyena mask, made by the Bamana people, c. 19th century, wood and metal.

claim that he guards his business jealously, and will not tolerate anyone else trying to get in on his scheme.

In Nigerian legends, witches can turn themselves into hyenas, a belief so entrenched within the traditional lore of the Bornu people of the northeast that their language even contains a special word, *bultungin*, which translates as 'I change

Hyena headdress, made by the Bamana people, *c.* 19th century, wood, metal, cane and cotton string.

myself into a hyena.' Hyena-wise, in fact, Nigeria – like Ethiopia – is a particularly interesting place. In 2005 an anonymous Brazilian contributor to Scamorama – a website devoted to exposing Nigerian e-mail frauds – sent in some pictures from Lagos, taken on a mobile phone, of men walking muzzled hyenas down a city street. The photographer assumed that the men were either robbers, thugs or debt collectors, adding: 'I don't know these guys (THANK GOD) but . . . one had an original gold Rolex so he must do some kind of ugly business I guess.' These images, published on the Scamorama website, attracted enormous attention, were circulated internationally, and have been reprinted in various places, including the CD insert of the Gorillaz album *Demon Days* and the cover of Martin Cohen's book *No Holiday: 80 Places You Don't Want to Visit* (2006). Wherever the pictures were published, it was broadly implied – and often directly stated – that in Nigeria hyenas were sometimes kept as pets or used as attack dogs, or were enlisted as muscle to help with criminal activities.

The South African photographer Pieter Hugo first came upon these photographs when they were published in his local newspaper under the headline 'The Streets of Lagos'. Fascinated by the images, Hugo decided to find out all he could about these ominous men and their muzzled companions. Through a

Hyena man. Mobile phone photo taken by an anonymous tourist, published on the Scamorama website in 2005.

journalist friend, he managed to track down a Nigerian reporter named Adetokunbo Abiola who promised to introduce Hugo to the *gadawan kura* (hyena handlers). After following a long trail, Hugo and Abiola made contact with the men, who were living in a shantytown in Dei Dei Junction, on the outskirts of Abuja. Hugo and Abiola tell their story in *The Hyena and Other Men* (2007). Contrary to rumour, it turned out that the hyena men were neither drug dealers nor debt collectors, but a family of travelling minstrels (a group of men and a little girl) who entertained crowds with their three spotted hyenas (Jamis, Mainasara and Gumu), four baboons and a number of rock pythons. The Ahmadu family practise a tradition, handed down through generations, of performing sensational, dervish-like feats such as walking on glowing hot coals and holding red-hot instruments in their hands. In addition to taming wild animals, the men sold samples of the amulets and herbal medicines that, they claimed, made them safe from danger.

Hugo's photographs are not the first record of the Nigerian tradition of hyena men. Almost a hundred years ago, an article by Major Arthur J. N. Tremearne was published in the anthropological journal *Man* entitled 'Nigerian Strolling Players'. In this article, Tremearne described the performers as 'clothed in a dress of patches and charms' and accompanied by one or more hyenas, which were exhibited in order to collect money and frighten children; 'the people deny that there is any religious significance in it'.[23] Unlike the subjects of Hugo's portraits, which seem artificial and staged in comparison, none of the performers in Tremearne's photographs, taken by W. A. Trumper, acknowledge the camera; the man holding the hyena is fully turned away. The casual composition and textual framing of this image suggest a measure of spontaneity that Hugo's more carefully posed images clearly lack.

In Hugo's account, Abdullahi Ahmadu explained to the jour-
nalists how his grandfather had initiated him into the secret of
immunity from hyenas, a ritual that involved capturing and
taming a hyena of his own. First, Abdullahi said, he both drank
and bathed in a protective potion that made him invisible to
hyenas. He then travelled with his family to the northern caves
and, at night, followed his hunting dogs to a hyena's lair, where
the men chanted magic incantations until the beast emerged.
Abdullahi then blew clouds of tranquillizing powder in the
animal's face. It struggled and fought, he said, but once the
medicine began to work, it started to obey.

The men's captured hyenas are kept in specially constructed
boxes, muzzled, and walked on thick, heavy chains. According

W. A. Trumper,
*Nigerian Strolling
Players*, before
1914, photograph,
first published in
Man, vol. XIV.

Pieter Hugo,
*Abdullahi Mohammed
with Mainasara,
Ogre-Remo, Nigeria,*
2007, C-print.

to Abdullahi, a hyena needs only one to two months of training in order to learn to live with humans and other animals, a process that involves the use of herbs, powders, amulets and esoteric incantations. Some of these magic charms are placed inside *akayau* – metal rings tied around the men's ankles that protect them from harm and help them to dance. The hyenas are fed on scraps purchased from the abattoir, plus a dead goat

every three days or so. 'We use a heavy stick to hit the hyenas on the head when they misbehave', said Abdullahi. 'We knock them down on the ground. All of us hold the sticks in case the animals become aggressive.'

The *gadawan kura* believe that their charms, concoctions and incantations make them invulnerable to hyena attacks. One of Hugo's more disturbing photographs shows Abdullahi's

Pieter Hugo, *Mummy Ahmadu and Mallam Mantari Lamal with Mainasara, Abuja, Nigeria*, 2005, C-print.

six-year-old daughter, Mummy, sitting astride the back of a large hyena. 'She cannot be harmed', said Abdullahi. 'She has taken a potion of traditional herbs and has been bathed with it. So her safety from the animals is guaranteed for the rest of her life.' In the city streets, the hyena men play with their animals and sell charms to onlookers that allow them to do the same; these charms are also said to protect against the curses and spells that many Nigerians believe are responsible for their misfortunes. In some respects, then, the performance of the *gadawan kura* reinforces the hyena's reputation as hostile, evil and possibly infernal in origin.

In Hugo's photographs, the hyenas are bound with woven muzzles attached to thick, heavy chains, and some of the men are depicted with sticks or clubs. The possibility of barely suppressed animal violence erupting is obviously what makes these hyenas compelling spectacles – or effective partners in crime. Their role in the act is to behave like savage and untamable creatures that have temporarily become placid, thereby endorsing the power of the charms, potions and amulets on sale. Significantly, however, Hugo notes that every one of the hyena men had scars on his face, legs and hands.

In 2005 Hugo and Abiola spent eight days travelling with the *gadawan kura*; they returned again in 2007 to take more photographs. The resulting images, exhibited in galleries worldwide, can also be seen on Hugo's website (www.pieterhugo.com). Interestingly, the photographer chose not to picture the men in the city streets where they plied their trade; instead, he shows them posing with their animals in bleak, wasteland settings – on a dusty backstreet, under a massive flyover, in a stretch of wilderness behind factories with broken windows. The titles of the photographs include the names of both the humans and animals depicted, along with a reference to the various cities in

Nigeria where the images were taken. The portraits imply that a new kind of trans-species relationship is emerging in these bleak zones of poverty and uncontrolled urbanization. Critic Will Smith points out that

> the compositions isolate individual men and animals in an otherwise depopulated landscape of shantytowns and highway overpasses. These are spaces in flux: streets and concrete houses appear to be either under construction or already in ruins. The partial infrastructure suggests an equally incomplete consolidation of the codes and conventions of urban life.[24]

The choice of backdrop not only makes the hyenas seem all the more totemic, but also emphasizes the in-between-ness of the hyenas, as well as their handlers. Both men and beasts, the photographs seem to imply, are unwanted creatures reduced to lives of scavenging on the margins of society, living every day with the simmering threat of repressed violence. As Smith explains, these images 'demand an understanding of political and social marginalization that can accommodate relationships of interdependency between humans and animals, even one as improbable as that between hyenas and men'.[25]

Hugo's portraits provoke anxiety and unease. Nevertheless, the hyena men's distinctive dress – ankle-length gowns of decorative patchwork, faded tank tops, acid-washed muscle shirts and vinyl flip-flops – was taken up by French fashion designer Olivier Borde in his 2010 Spring/Summer collection, entitled 'Brutality in Pale Colors'. The collection is inspired, according to the designer's press release, 'by the almost post-urban mood of the Pieter Hugo series The Hyena Men, which features conversely tranquil and ferocious animals leashed at the neck and led by

Pieter Hugo,
*Abdullahi
Mohammed with
Mainasara, Lagos,
Nigeria*, 2007,
C-print.

young men dressed in multiple layers of soft, used, dusty and pale-colored clothing'. For those unable to afford the main items in the collection, the designer also offers hand-dyed linen tote bags printed with a sketch of a muzzled hyena slavering at the chops, and a 'destroyed hyena tee' – a threadbare, torn, shredded T-shirt printed with the same image (designed, presumably, to look as though it has been chewed up by a spotted hyena) – which retails for around £150, probably more than the *gadawan kura* make in a year.

4 Wargs and Scrunts

I sniff a broken drum. I bristle. My pelt is silver.
I howl my song to the moon – up it goes.
Would you meet me there in the waste places?
Edwin Morgan, 'Hyena', 1990

Macarius of Alexandria was a monk who, until his death in 395, lived alone in the Nitrian desert in Egypt. One day, according to legend, a female hyena approached the ascetic in his monastic retreat, bearing a newly born blind cub in her mouth. The pious saint, taking pity on this unfortunate beast, touched the eyes of the cub, causing it – miraculously – to see. The mother hyena was so grateful that the following morning she brought St Macarius a freshly killed sheep, only to be reprimanded by the holy man, who admonished her that he never ate anything that had been killed with violence, and neither should she. As the story has it, from that day forth, the humble hyena laid off meat entirely and visited the saint in his cell every morning, where she was permitted to share his bread. In this story, a variant on the well-known parable of St Francis and the wolf, the hyena functions to show the saint's humility and peaceful virtue – he is modest enough to perform a miracle for the sake of a mere hyena (and what a lucky beast she was, to be given a saint's leftover crusts every day instead of her usual daily diet of fresh meat).

The hyena's role in this parable is to highlight certain qualities in the saint. This is typical of most hyena-themed literature; when hyenas are mentioned, they rarely matter in their own right. Invariably, they are metaphors or symbols representing savagery,

Hyenas Quarrelling over their Prey, 1887, engraving.

'Striped Hyenas', from Gaston Maspero, *A History of Egypt* (1895–7).

desolation, ferocity, cowardice or some similar unpleasant tendency in human beings.

In the Hebrew Bible, the word for hyena – *tzebua* or *zevoa* (literally 'howling creature') – is used four times. In 1 Samuel 13:18, we learn of the 'Valley of Zevoim', widely believed to be a valley north of Jericho known in Arabic as *Shaqq-ud-Diba* ('cleft of the hyenas') or *Wadi-Abu-Diba* ('valley of the hyenas'). 'Is my heritage unto me as the hyena's den?', laments the prophet rhetorically in Jeremiah 12:9. In other words, just as the hyena makes its home in the sepulchres of the dead, the prophet's birthright has been taken over by others, and his suffering and pain represent the plight of all Israel. In the book of ethical teachings known as *Ecclesiasticus* or *The Wisdom of Sirach*, another rhetorical question is asked: 'What peace is there between the hyena and the dog? And what peace between the rich man and the poor?' Elsewhere, in the Epistle of Barnabas (and, according to some versions, in Deuteronomy 16:7), we are reminded not to eat the meat of the hyena, also known simply as 'the Brute'.

In his *Metamorphoses*, Ovid, quoting Pythagoras, takes up the notion of hyenas as hermaphrodites, and uses them to introduce the concept of sexual transition. 'We might marvel at how the hyena changes function, and how a female, taken from behind by a male, is now a male', Pythagoras observes, inaccurately.[1] In English literature of the Renaissance, the hyena is characterized either as a lustful hermaphrodite or an evil hypocrite, and sometimes both. An attribute often associated with the hyena at this time was spots, and a common trope among literary authors of the Renaissance was to use spotted animals to evoke duplicity, evil and deceit. A typical example is found in book three of *The Faerie Queene* (1590), where a witch conjures up a 'hideous beast, of horrible aspect'. This creature's 'backe' is 'spect / With thousand spots of colours quaint elect', giving it a resemblance to the 'Hyena' – used here to embody the quality of lust – 'That feeds on wemens flesh, as others feede on grass.'[2] To Renaissance readers, the hyena would have been regarded as a monstrous hybrid frequently associated with witches and witchcraft, as well as a voracious man-eater (or, here, woman-eater) that violates the norms of nature. Spenser also implies that the beast has the ability to speak, suggesting that it trespasses into the human realm, which, paradoxically, serves to make it even more monstrous.

In *Euphues: The Anatomy of Wit* (1578), the playwright John Lyly reprises the old superstition that the hyena is hermaphroditic – or, at least, malevolently deceptive – by referring to it as a two-faced female creature who 'when she speaketh like a man deviseth most mischief'.[3] In Shakespeare's *As You Like It* (1623), the disguised Rosalind, in a feigned attempt to cure Orlando of his love, informs him they are so mismatched that she will 'laugh like a hyena, when thou art inclined to sleep'.[4] On one hand, by comparing herself to the allegedly promiscuous hyena, Rosalind could be trying to elicit Orlando's reaction to the idea of being cuckolded. On the other hand, since she is dressed as a boy at the time, she could be referring to the hyena's hermaphroditic tendencies, trying to find out how Orlando would feel about finding a young man in his bed. The hyena is also alluded to in Milton's *Samson Agonistes* (1671), where Samson denounces Dalila for her falseness and feminine wiles with the words 'Out, out, Hyaena! These are thy wonted arts, / And arts of every woman false like thee – / To break all faith, all vows, deceive, betray'.[5] Milton refers again to the hyena in his *Pro se Defensio* (1655), when he charges the Calvinist preacher Alexander More with vicious hypocrisy. 'Hyena!', he says, 'or if there is any beast so noxious and infamous with loathsome fraud!'[6] It seems there is not.

In the Jacobean satire *Eastward Ho* (1605), by George Chapman, Ben Jonson and John Marston, a character named Touchstone declares his steadfastness by resolving: 'I will neither yield to the song of the siren nor the voice of the hyena'.[7] The Restoration poet John Dryden, in his play *The Conquest of Granada* (1672), pairs the hyena with the allegedly mendacious crocodile; both are notoriously deceitful creatures. The Moorish king Abdelmelech says of the lovely but devious Lyndaraxa: 'I'll sooner trust th'hyena than your smile; / Or, than your tears, the weeping crocodile.'[8]

It was, presumably, for similarly duplicitous tendencies that, three years after the publication of *A Vindication of the Rights of Woman* (1792), Horace Walpole, in a private letter, memorably described Mary Wollstonecraft as 'a hyena in petticoats'. Perhaps echoing Walpole's phrase, Charlotte Brontë, in a fascinating metaphor that plays both openly and covertly with transgressed expectations of femininity, describes the unfortunate Bertha

Mason – the 'madwoman in the attic' in *Jane Eyre* (1847) – as a 'clothed hyena' that 'rose up and stood tall on its hind feet'.[9]

In the modern age, the hyena continues to function as a yardstick by which to measure our own nastiest qualities. Inspired by the tragedy of the Boer War, Rudyard Kipling's 1919 poem 'The Hyaenas' contrasts the animals that scavenge on the freshly buried dead with those critics and commentators who condemned the war as unjust. The hyenas that unearth the body of a hastily buried soldier, observed the poet, do not concern themselves about 'how he died and why he died'; they simply 'snout the bushes and stones aside / And dig till they come to it'.[10] Being soulless, the hyenas are 'free from shame' – unlike those who criticize the war, who not only abuse the dead but also 'defile the dead man's name'. In wartime, argues Kipling in this angry poem, the hyena looks honest in comparison to certain vile specimens of humanity.

Even here, however, the hyena is being used as a symbol, evoking the very worst tendencies of the animal world. Only the lowest forms of our own species can compare. 'In shooting a burglar, do not feel that you are taking a human life', advised a 1902 article on 'etiquette' in the Pennsylvania newspaper the *Reading Eagle*. Why not? Because 'the burglar is a human hyena, and as all the animal kingdom despise the hyena, so ought the higher intellectual animals regard the burglar'.[11]

Hyenas feature prominently in the work of the Surrealist artist and author Leonora Carrington, who sometimes painted herself as a hyena, or as accompanied by one. It is not clear whether Carrington associated the hyena with female sexuality, but it is certain that this was her totem animal, and she connected it with transformation and freedom from the stifling domesticity of aristocratic life. This theme is evident in her strange and disturbing short story 'The Debutante', written during 1937–8 when the artist was twenty-two and living in Paris with her lover, Max Ernst. In this very brief, surreal tale, the narrator, an unhappy young debutante who loathes parties, befriends a sly female hyena at the local zoo. The hyena offers to take her place at a coming-out ball, and suggests she be allowed to tear off the face of the debutante's maid and wear it as a disguise. The debutante agrees, but the plan fails, because the hyena's smell gives her away. The end of the story is shocking and odd:

> My mother came in, pale with fury. 'We had just sat down to eat', she said, 'when that thing in your place gets up and cries, "I smell a bit strong, eh? Well I don't eat cake."' Then she tore off her face and ate it. With one bound she disappeared through the window.[12]

'Brown hyena', from Pierre Boitard and G. Barba, *Le jardin des plantes: description et moeurs des mammifères de la ménagerie et du Museum d'Histoire Naturelle, Paris* (1851).

'The Debutante' was made into a short, haunting film by Ric Warren (1994), which extends the tale by filling out the text with extracts from Carrington's journals and other autobiographical writings. The soundtrack consists of extracts from Ravel's dreamy tone poem, *Daphnis and Chloé*.

Hyenas crop up here and there in twentieth-century literature, most often in works with exotic, jungle or fantasy settings. In such texts, hyenas generally stand as generic threats to the protagonist, though some authors use them for different reasons. One of the doctor's most formidable creatures in H. G. Wells's

Leonora Carrington, *Self-portrait*, 1936.

William Daniell, Striped hyena with erect mane and the requisite bones, 1807, engraving.

The Island of Dr Moreau (1896) is a cross between a hyena and a swine. Jack London's hyenas in *Before Adam* (1906) are wise and crafty, though still threatening. Unsurprisingly perhaps, hyenas are frequently mentioned in Edgar Rice Burroughs's Tarzan books. In *Tarzan and the Mark of the Red Hyena* (1967), the native leader Bukawai the Unclean ties Tarzan to a stake and leaves him to be eaten alive by hyenas, two of which accompany the dastardly Bukawai wherever he goes. In the Tarzan movies, however, hyenas are often discussed but rarely seen – though their whooping laughter is sometimes heard on the soundtrack (in the 1932 film *Tarzan the Ape Man*, Tarzan's trademark yell is, improbably, mistaken for the laugh of a hyena).

In *Out of Africa*, by Isak Dinesen (1937), a Danish traveller to Hamburg, Count Schimmelmann, happens to come across a small, itinerant menagerie and is especially interested in its hyena. The zoo's proprietor approaches him and gives him some unasked-for information about this exotic animal. 'It is a great thing to have got a Hyena to Hamburg, where there has never been one till now', explains the zookeeper. 'All Hyenas, you will know, are hermaphrodites, and in Africa, where they come from, on a full-moon night they will meet and join in a ring of copulation wherein each individual takes the double part of male and female. Did you know that?' The Count, 'with a slight movement of disgust', admits that he did not.[13]

In 2001 a hyena played an important role in Yann Martel's fantasy adventure *The Life of Pi*. In this fable-like novel, the protagonist, Pi, is cast adrift in a lifeboat with a zebra, a spotted hyena, an orang-utan and a huge Bengal tiger named Richard Parker. A battle for survival ensues on the cramped boat, and Pi struggles to avoid being part of the animals' food chain. Unlike the noble tiger that the hero comes to love, the unnamed spotted hyena is depicted as frightening and cowardly, and Pi is eager for him to die. First, the hyena saves its own skin by putting the zebra between the tiger and itself; next, it eats the dying zebra alive; finally, it kills Orange Juice, an orang-utan that Pi has come to be fond of.

As the butt of cautionary tales, hyenas have proved useful in folklore, poetry and – notably – children's books. A brief sample of titles shows how they come across: *The Mean Hyena*, *The Tale of Harry the Heartless Hyena*, *Hungry Hyena*, *The Greedy Hyena*, *The Foolish Hyena*, *Tasmin and the Wicked Hyena*. Typical of the genre is *Sophocles the Hyena: A Fable* by Jim Moran, with illustrations by Andy Warhol. In this book, Sophocles, an evil-natured hyena, is given lion chops to eat, which leads him to become friendly and give up his nasty habit of trying to eat cats. Popular illustrator Richard Scarry's recurring cast of animal characters includes Harry the Hyena, a layabout who spends his time basking in the sun or getting into trouble with his pals Wolfgang Wolf and Benny Baboon.

Andy Warhol,
from Jim Moran,
*Sophocles the
Hyena* (1954).

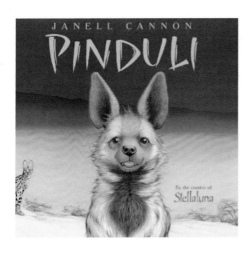

In this context, *Pinduli* (2004), a book by Jannell Cannon for children aged four to eight, makes a refreshing change. The book tells the story of Pinduli, a baby striped hyena who is teased by the other animals for her big ears, fuzzy mane and striped skin, despite the fact that her mother tells her she is 'the most beautiful hyena ever'. Pinduli teaches the other animals a lesson in prejudice and public perception by disguising herself as a ghost. Cannon describes her book as 'a triumphant story about self-image, self-acceptance, and treating others with respect' and explains that, in Swahili, Pinduli means 'catalyst for great change or cause of change'.[14]

POPULAR CULTURE

In 1946 Al Capp's syndicated US newspaper cartoon strip *L'il Abner* introduced its readers to Lena the Hyena, otherwise known as 'the ugliest woman in the world'. So hideous was Lena that she appeared in the comic strip as a blank space. Capp

Basil Wolverton, Lena the Hyena, 'The Ugliest Woman in the World', from Al Capp's *L'il Abner* comic strip (1946).

declared Lena to be so ugly that he was unable to draw her image himself. In an extraordinarily successful publicity stunt, he enlisted readers to send in their own drawings. Boris Karloff, Salvador Dalí and Frank Sinatra were contest judges, and over 500,000 readers sent in their impressions. The winner turned out to be Basil Wolverton, who later became a famous cartoonist in his own right; his version of Lena was a grotesque creature with prominent horse's teeth set in a hyena's drooling jaws.

As this anecdote amply testifies, hyenas in pop culture are most often cast in the role of the villain or dupe. Usually, they are depicted as laughing idiots, hysterical and unhinged. In *Batman: The Animated Series*, a spin-off that aired on Fox between 1992 and 1995, the Joker owns two identical, unnamed pet hyenas with red collars who are looked after by his girlfriend, Harley Quinn, who refers to them as her 'babies'. In *The New Batman Adventures*, a second spin-off series that aired on Warner

Brothers from 1997 until 1999, the twin hyenas are referred to as Bud and Lou, after the comedians Abbott and Costello. Six years later, in March 2005, Bud and Lou reappeared as characters in the children's cartoon series *Krypto the Superdog*, which premiered on the Cartoon Network. Here the twin laughing hyenas function as the primary foes of Batman's pet dog, Ace the Bat-Hound, constantly trying to thwart him using props given them by their master, the Joker. In one episode, for example, Bud has a joy-buzzer under his collar that gives off electric shocks, and in another the hyenas use a bubble shooter that fires 'giggle bubbles', causing their victims to laugh uncontrollably. Both hyenas have a distinctive odour; in one episode, Ace observes to Krypto that he can 'smell their evil'.

Today, however, most young people come to know (or think they know) about hyenas from watching the Disney movie *The Lion King*, which was released in 1994 and enjoyed great popularity in its animated form and later as a Broadway musical. Since this fatuous story continues to exert an enormous influence over the public perception of hyenas, and is the basis, in part, of their bad reputation, it is worth considering in some detail.

As part of their pre-production research for this enormously successful animated film, a handful of Disney studio artists spent two days observing and sketching the captive spotted hyenas at the Field Station for Behavioral Research in the hills above the University of California's Berkeley campus. The two scientists who agreed to the visit, Laurence Frank and Stephen Glickman, both made a strong request to the artists that the film's depiction of hyenas be a positive one. According to Glickman, the artists responded that the script was out of their hands, as it had already been written. They went on to explain that the three hyenas, Banzai, Shenzi and Ed, were to be the allies of Scar, an older lion who would eventually lose out to the hero, a handsome younger lion named Simba. However, the scientists were reassured that the three hyenas would be comical characters rather than positively evil.

Whether the hyena trio is funny is a matter of opinion, but they are certainly far from innocuous. While the lion heroes (voiced by James Earl Jones and Jeremy Irons) are dignified and philosophical, the hyenas are made to seem foolish and ridiculous. Shenzi, the dominant hyena (voiced by Whoopi Goldberg), is a female. We know this because she lacks the dark grey 'stubble' that adorns the snouts of the two males; she sports a prominent fringe hanging over her face; and she has dark patches round her eyes shaped to resemble heavily applied eye shadow. The middle hyena, the short-fused Banzai (voiced by Cheech Marin), is belligerent and greedy, constantly looking for food and a fight. The youngest of the three, Ed (voiced by Jim Cummings), seems mentally retarded; cross-eyed and apparently unable to speak like the other animals, his tongue lolls out of his mouth, and when not laughing crazily he sports a huge, vacant grin. There seem to be pieces missing from his ears, and his mane has been reduced to a small cowlick.

The hyena trio lives in a place known as the Elephant's Graveyard, located at the nether border of the so-called Pride Land, where the lions live. They have formed an alliance with the Lion King's evil and effete brother Scar (voiced by Irons), whom they serve in return for meat. In one of the film's most remarkable musical numbers, a song called 'Be Prepared', Scar, perched on a high cliff, oversees an army of goose-stepping hyenas marching in the valley below him, a sequence clearly modelled after footage from Leni Riefenstahl's Nazi propaganda movie *Triumph of the Will* (1935). On the original soundtrack recording of *The Lion King*, Scar begins his musical number following a soliloquy in which he meditates on the 'crude and unspeakably plain' nature of hyenas. In the film, however, these lines are cut, and Scar, addressing his troops, gets straight to the point, informing the gathered mass of hyenas that they are 'wet', 'thick' and 'vacant', and that 'the lights are not all on upstairs'.

Scar's evil scheme to take over the kingdom succeeds, at least for a while, and when his nephew Simba leaves the Pride Land after the death of his father, Scar succeeds to the throne. Years later, after learning the hard facts about the so-called Circle of Life, Simba returns to his father's kingdom as a full-grown lion, only to find the Pride Land in shadow. Under Scar's reign, bones lie scattered everywhere; yes, the filthy hyenas have trashed the place.

Unsurprisingly, this depiction did not impress the Berkeley biologists. In his conclusion to a spotted hyena fact sheet written for *African Geographic* in May 2006, Laurence Frank suggested that boycotting all screenings of *The Lion King* would be a useful way of helping to preserve hyenas in the wild. Stephen Glickman concluded, stoically, that 'these are not new images of hyenas. Their portrayal in contemporary media as weird, dangerous, repulsive animals, with a few recent exceptions, has been quite consistent.'[15]

Some critics suggested that *The Lion King* had racist undertones. It did not go unnoticed that the hyenas all speak in African American or Latino accents (and are played by African American and Latino actors), whereas the noble lions all have British or American voices. In an article published in the film journal *Jump Cut* entitled 'A Short History of Disney-fascism' (1996), cultural analyst Matt Roth describes the hyenas as 'a teeming brood of half-starved scavengers ghettoized in a "dark region"'.[16] Of their neighbourhood, he writes:

The huge elephant skeletons resemble the burnt-out shells of tall buildings, or perhaps the postindustrial remains of hulking machinery. Simba, on a dare, starts to enter a huge skull, only to be frozen in his tracks by eerie laughter. In classic hooligan fashion, three hyenas emerge and start circling Simba, taunting and threatening him. It's clear that Simba is on the wrong side of the tracks, in a bad neighborhood, surrounded by 'the projects' – he's caught in the inner city.[17]

The film's greatest infelicity, however, is its representation of spotted hyenas – which, according to Jane Goodall, who is widely considered to be one of the world's foremost experts on spotted hyenas, are just as intelligent as primates – as gibbering idiots, their silliness epitomized by Ed, the drooling mute, who is so dense that at one point he gnaws on his own leg, mistaking it for a chop. The image recalls Hemingway's hyena in *Green Hills of Africa*, running round in circles and eating his own intestines after being shot. Here the hyena appears as Ourobouros, the snake devouring its own tail, the degraded animal that destroys even itself.

Incidentally, hyenas have been known to chew themselves, but only when suffering in captivity at the hands of human captors. On 23 September 1910 *The New York Times* reported that a hyena – 'not of the laughing variety' – was 'committing progressive suicide' in the National Zoological Garden in Washington, DC. By the time zookeepers discovered the apparently demented animal, it had gnawed off one of its own legs 'from paw to knee joint' and was said to be drinking its own blood. This is hardly surprising; the hyena is a very intelligent animal, and plenty of human beings commit suicide at the prospect of spending the rest of their lives behind bars. 'Several years ago at the zoo, a

In the 1930s this striped hyena in Tel Aviv Zoo was taken for a walk each day in the courtyard.

hyena chewed its side until several ribs were exposed', reported the article, concluding stoically: 'it was shot'.[18]

Elsewhere in popular culture, hyenas appear in the thin disguise of evil mythical creatures with unappealing names. In Norse mythology, the word *warg* is used to describe the mythical wolf Fenrir and his sons Skoll and Hati. In *The Lord of the Rings*, J.R.R. Tolkien uses the word to refer to a wolf-like creature of a particularly evil kind. When Peter Jackson filmed his *Lord of the Rings* movie trilogy, however, he turned Tolkien's wargs into creatures that look far more like giant spotted hyenas than they do wolves. In interviews, Jackson explained that the new design was chosen to make the creatures look more threatening and powerful. The wargs in the film have thick muscles tensioned around the jaw, neck and front end, forming creatures that look as if they could easily incapacitate anyone with a single, well-placed bite. And in M. Night Shyamalan's film *Lady in the Water* (2006), the inhabitants of a Philadelphia apartment building find themselves assailed by 'scrunts' – hyena-like creatures with glowing red eyes

Yu-Gi-Oh! Trading Card Game, hyena card from 1996.

Una Fricker, 'Gibbering Hyena' card, from *Magic: The Gathering*, 1996.

and thick, grassy fur, which allows them to hide undetected in lawns and bushes, stalking the human beings they prey on.

Hyena hybrids also lurk in the gaming subculture, playing a significant role in the manga game *Yu-Gi-Oh!* and, more significantly, in *World of Warcraft*, where explorers may encounter fearsome hyenas with names like Snort the Heckler, Hecklefang Snarler, Steelsnap, Starving Snickerfang, Rabid Blisterpaw and Maraudine Bonepaw. These skinnable, carnivorous beasts are, like the hyenas in *The Lion King*, found only in the bleakest territories – places with names like The Barrens, Desolace, Tanaris, Dire Maul, Blasted Lands, Dragon Blight, Western Plaguelands and Thousand Needles. They have the ability to inflict dangerous diseases on those who fight them and are sometimes used as attack animals, but may also be kept as 'ferocity pets'.

Gibbering hyenas   2🟢

Summon Hyenas

Gibbering Hyenas cannot block black creatures.

Hyenas laughing—what's the joke?
—Femeref phrase meaning
"that's not funny"

Illus. Una Fricker   3/2
©1996 Wizards of the Coast, Inc. All rights reserved.

Like jackals and vultures, hyenas are often used as metaphors to represent those who are widely considered among the lowest ranks of humanity – crooked politicians, ambulance-chasing lawyers, money-grubbing bankers and shady paparazzi. The recent financial meltdown has generated a lot of talk about 'hedge fund hyenas', with disgraced investor Bernard Madoff prominent among the tribe. Men who prey on other men's women are also sometimes rewarded with the comparison. In 1996 Mark Leyner's back-page column in *Esquire*, intended as a comic riff on the Disney movie, was called 'The Hyena King'. The thrust of Leyner's joke was that hyenas make better role models than lions because 'the lion expends tremendous time and energy grimly chasing his prey. The hyena, laughing maniacally, feasts effortlessly on pre-killed carrion.' The satirist's advice? 'Let your brother play the lion and spend weeks, months, perhaps even years pursuing and courting his wife. You be the hyena and tryst insouciantly with her against a cigarette machine in the bowels of some catering hall at a family reunion.'[19]

It is worth thinking a little more carefully about the use of animals as metaphors to express (generally undesirable) traits in the human species. John Berger, in his essay 'Why Look at Animals?', makes a characteristically acute observation about the French caricaturist J. J. Grandville's illustrations of dogs (and in many ways, it seems, the hyena is so difficult for us to get a handle on because it so closely resembles the much-venerated dog). Berger observes that Grandville's dogs are not being 'borrowed' to explain people. Indeed, quite the contrary:

> These animals have become prisoners of a human/social situation into which they have been press-ganged. The vulture as landlord is more dreadfully rapacious than he is as a bird. The crocodiles at dinner are greedier at the table than they are in the river. Here, animals are not being used as reminders of origin, or as moral metaphors, they are being used *en masse* to people situations. The movement that ends with the banality of Disney began as a disturbing, prophetic dream in the work of Grandville.[20]

When a human being is described as a 'hyena', in other words, we can be sure it is due to behaviour that is more offensive and egregious than anything found in the animal world, where competition is, for the most part, an honest and straightforward battle for survival. Since they are so rarely seen in real life, at least in the West, hyenas can be used in this way because they are a blank screen, suited to the projection of our own anxieties and concerns. And the more we talk about symbolic hyenas, the less it

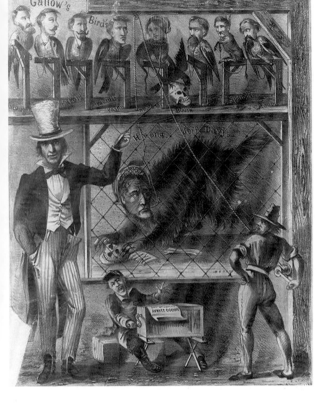

Uncle Sam's Menagerie, 1865, lithograph on woven paper. This illustration was issued in the wake of Lincoln's assassination in April 1865, and conveys some of the public hostility toward the conspirators, whom the public associated with the former president of the Confederacy, Jefferson Davis. Uncle Sam stands before a cage in which a hyena with the bonneted head of Jefferson Davis claws at a skull.

matters to us that real hyenas are becoming increasingly scarce. Our indifference toward their increasingly endangered status has nothing to do with hyenas themselves, and everything to do with the way we use them to reflect our own worst qualities. Perhaps this is one reason why hyenas are not popular in zoos. Confronted with a shy, gentle creature when they are expecting a stupid, snickering scavenger, human visitors might well get the feeling they have been cheated.

5 Bad Rap

> It was a spotted hyena, the kind people think of when they hear the word 'hyena' – a dirty, matted creature dripping with blood.
>
> Joanna Greenfield, 'Hyena', *New Yorker*, 1996

In Europe and the US, where there are no wild hyenas to be found (and very few in captivity), hyenas are still very unpopular animals. Partly, of course, this is due to the context in which they are presented. Wildlife documentaries and safari footage inevitably show hyenas living up to their reputation by preying on other animals or feasting after a kill. When rolling around inside the decaying carcass of an elephant or munching nonchalantly on the spine of a still-struggling buffalo, hyenas can seem very nasty indeed. Since their social lives are spent largely in burrows underground, rarely do we see documentary footage of hyena cubs playing together, mothers feeding their young, clan members nuzzling affectionately or any other activity that might make them seem less repellent to the public eye. No doubt about it: the hyena has a bad rap.

HYENA HATRED

Such widespread aversion to a creature that is virtually never encountered deserves further consideration. After much thought, I can come up with no other animal whose reputation is so at odds with the reality, not even the rat, which, despite widespread dislike, has many admirers, and apparently makes a charming pet. Hyenas are not reptiles or invertebrates – the

A snarling striped hyena, with erect mane, looking especially threatening and demonic.

usual kinds of creatures that incite widespread disgust – but are furry, warm-blooded mammals that nurse their young (and, in this, there are some parallels between our feelings about the hyena and our feelings about other ambiguous carnivores such as the jackal and the wolf). Surely very few of those people who claim to despise hyenas can have lived through a traumatic encounter with one, even at a zoo. And why are hyenas so reviled when in many respects they look very similar to dogs, which are widely beloved? Most people's aversion to hyenas, clearly, has less to do with real hyenas than the context in which they are generally depicted, the misinformation that circulates about their habits and – as with rats and bats – the things they are associated with. There are five possible reasons for the degradation of hyenas: their evolutionary role, their status as scavengers, their aesthetic qualities, their temperaments and their association with death.

First, since the aversion to hyenas seems to be so widespread, it is worth considering whether it might be rooted in evolutionary selection pressures. Ecologist Marcus Baynes-Rock, who has spent time studying the urbanized hyenas in the Ethiopian city of Harar, believes that our instinctive aversion is a result of co-evolution. Both humans and hyenas, he notes, are social predators that evolved on the savannah of Africa, scavenging from the kills of lions and sabre-toothed cats. 'For 3.5 million years, hyenas and other groups of hominins have been our direct competition and no doubt greatest threats', observes Baynes-Rock. 'Look at bone assemblages from the Plio-Pleistocene period, and there will be cut marks from stone tools mixed up with toothmarks from hyenas. Chances are, the prey was killed by a capable hunter (probably cat, not human) and then fought over by hominins and hyenas.'[1] For those with faith in evolutionary psychology, our adaptive history cannot be overlooked.

The striped hyena depicted as a scavenging capitalist, *Harper's Weekly* (December 1894).

Secondly, it has been argued that hyenas are reviled because they are scavengers – neither hunters nor prey, they occupy an ambiguous role in our cultural scheme. Many believe this is why scavengers, like other outsiders, are considered terrifying and taboo. It is true that hyenas are remarkably efficient scavengers; indeed, their jaws and digestive systems are uniquely adapted to this very purpose. Yet, few people know that spotted

An angry-looking spotted hyena shows its teeth.

hyenas are also skilful predators, and regularly hold their own against lions. In fact, when it comes down to it, lions scavenge from hyenas far more often than hyenas from lions, but we seldom hear lions described as scavengers. Stephen Glickman, an expert on spotted hyenas, notes that when observers come upon hyenas feeding on a carcass, they immediately assume the animal has been killed by another predator, and the hyenas have moved in to pick over the remains. Similarly, when spotted hyenas are seen standing back from lions feeding on a kill, the immediate assumption is that the lions did all the hard work, and the hyenas are hanging around waiting to snatch a few scraps. Yet, explains Glickman, 'it is clear that the noble, much-admired king of beasts scavenges more often on hyena kills than hyenas scavenge on lion kills'.[2]

Still, scavengers do no harm; indeed, their importance to the environment is well known. Spotted hyenas are vital to the recycling of nutrients in their savannah ecosystem, and the Masai tribes in Kenya and Tanzania will often leave out their dead to be disposed of by them. Among African tribal cultures, there is nothing shameful about scavenging meat from lion kills; it is simply pragmatic. Indeed, scaring away the lions can be a very risky business. Nevertheless, in human society, especially under capitalism, productivity is considered the *sine qua non* of civilized achievement.

Thirdly, let us consider the question of the hyena's aesthetic qualities. The animal's 'ugliness' is surely a matter of opinion, though authors such as anthropologist Dan Boneh write as though it were a simple matter of fact. Here is Boneh, describing the spotted hyena:

Nature has given this animal a particularly ugly appearance. Its rough fur is coloured a shady grey or yellow spotted with brown dots. Its head is sturdy and disproportionate to a strong and bulky neck. Its back is usually lower than its front and, with its characteristically swollen stomach, it has a heavy, clumsy and unappealing appearance.[3]

True, hyenas have disproportionately large heads, but so do pandas and koala bears. The hyena's head, with its large ears, short, broad muzzle, thick neck and rounded skull, is carried low in relation to the body, but then, so is that of the beloved British bulldog, which shares with the hyena a powerful lower jaw. Hyenas have erectile manes, but so do lions and wolves. Their long back and short front legs give their bodies an asymmetrical quality, but kangaroos, bears and gorillas also have asymmetrical bodies, and they all have plenty of fans. Nor are hyenas themselves homogeneous. Spotted hyenas are as different from aardwolves as baboons from gorillas. Hyenas are unusual-looking creatures, true, but not as unusual as hedgehogs or armadillos. 'They definitely have bad-hair days, like all of us', admits zoologist Kay Holekamp of Michigan State University, who has studied hyenas in Kenya for more than fifteen years, 'but I find a lot of them quite beautiful.'[4]

Geoffrey Miller, an evolutionary psychologist at the University of New Mexico, claims that we find asymmetrical animals unattractive because we are obsessively vigilant for signs of ill health in others. He argues that asymmetry, like exaggerated, stunted or incomplete features, strikes us as a sign of sickness. Anything that 'looks rough and irregular when it should be smooth' is considered unappealing, claims Miller. 'Anything mottled is considered unattractive. Patchy hair is considered unattractive.'[5] On the other hand, beauty can be present by its violation, and a taste for the unconventional has always been seen as a mark of sophistication, a passage into the artistic vanguard.

As for the way they smell, those who work with hyenas admit that they can smell pretty rank up close, but a bad smell is not always enough to condemn an animal; the skunk is cute, popular, and sometimes even kept as a pet. Those familiar with hyenas report that their 'butter' smells like a pleasant, musky soap. To other hyenas, it is no doubt intoxicating. Expert

Stephen Glickman notes that hyenas smell far less strongly than lions, which are rarely accused of making a stink.

Fourthly, hyenas are reputed to have a malicious temperament, and are often believed to be stupid and cowardly; in fact, nothing could be further from the truth. Spotted hyenas in particular can be remarkably brave, taking down lions and zebras as well as wildebeest and other animals many times their size. On occasion, some especially bold hyena groups will join lions in their feed, sometimes even forcing the lions off the kill. In certain circumstances, moreover, spotted hyenas and lions will battle. If they come upon a group of feeding lionesses unaccompanied by males, spotted hyenas will usually drive the lionesses away. They will also steal the kills of cheetahs, which are easily intimidated, and leopards, which will sometimes put up a fight. Often, a pack of spotted hyenas will follow a pack of wild dogs, hoping to scavenge some of their prey. When the dogs are feeding after a kill, a solitary hyena might sneak up and try to make off with a piece of meat, though she does risk being mobbed. Actually, spotted hyenas make much better pirates when they work in groups. True, they hunt at night to avoid danger, and they employ 'feints' and 'tests' when hunting, but one might argue that such qualities testify to intelligence, rather than cowardice. As for the striped and brown hyenas, 'peaceful' and 'gentle' are the words that most readily come to mind. The small, insect-eating aardwolf is even monogamous, a rare quality among animals – and humans, too, for that matter.

They may seem malicious when chasing down a kill, but spotted hyenas, like dogs, can be readily domesticated if raised by hand from birth. An anonymous account published in *Harper's New Monthly Magazine* in 1853 tells of the author's time in Algeria, where he was given a young spotted hyena to keep as a pet. The animal 'soon became attached to me, after the manner of a faithful and gentle dog', we learn. 'This creature became the inseparable companion of my rambles . . . and with her I felt certain of never going astray.'[6] Hans Kruuk, the foremost authority on the spotted hyena, raised one as a house pet, and the faithful Solomon accompanied Professor Kruuk to Kenya on his research expeditions, sleeping peacefully beside him in his tent. 'Hyenas are very likable animals', observes Kruuk. 'They have such chubby, friendly faces.'[7] Finally, volume six of Charles Dickens's *Household Words*, published in 1853, contains an account of one Lieutenant-Colonel Sykes, who tamed a young hyena in India, brought it back with him to England, then gave it as a gift to the Royal Zoological Gardens in London. Sykes expected the animal would soon 'outgrow its early affection', but on his visits to the zoo, he discovered,

> it has always greeted me, not only as an old acquaintance, but as an old friend; and if I am to judge from its agitation and peculiar cries, the animal's recognition is that of affection. On Sunday last it was asleep in its cage when I approached. On calling it by its name it looked up, distinguished me in the crowd, started on its legs, and on my applying my hand to its mouth to smell, rubbed its head, neck, and back against my hand, then started on its legs and bounded about its cage, uttering short cries.[8]

The renowned zoologist Jane Goodall, speaking at Bristol's WildTalk series of lectures on the Great Apes in 2004, announced that if she had a chance to dedicate her life's work to another animal, it would be the spotted hyena. Along with her first husband, wildlife photographer Hugo von Lawick, Goodall is co-author of the book *Innocent Killers* (1971), which deals with spotted hyenas, jackals, African wild dogs and other predators.

From her work with spotted hyenas, Goodall has come to believe them to be among the most intelligent animals on earth. She points out that they are unusually clever, social creatures whose large, matriarchal clans are structured much more subtly than those of other carnivorous mammals. In fact, Goodall suggests that their social relationships are quite similar to those of baboons and mandrills, in that they relate to one another using all their senses, remembering such personal details as kin and rank, and using this information in social decision-making. In other words, not only do they recognize a fellow spotted hyena they might not have seen for a while, but they can remember how trustworthy she is and who her closest friends are.

Finally, hyenas, so the story goes, have filthy habits; after all, they feed on dead bodies, decaying flesh and even bones. It is true that hyenas have a long association with death and

'Striped Hyenas and Jackal', from Richard Lydekker, *Wild Life of the World* (1916).

dead bodies, which is perhaps where they first picked up their horror-movie reputation. From a right-to-life point of view, however, is it not less 'evil' to eat bodies that are already dead than to prey on live ones, as do lions and tigers? It is also true that hyenas have certainly been known to dig up corpses, but is this any more 'evil' an act than that of the family dog unearthing a long-forgotten bone?

Most human beings have a particularly archaic and animistic reaction to the notion of feeding off corpses, since, we believe, dead bodies have the tendency to pollute and corrupt everything they come into contact with. The only people for whom the sight of corpses provokes not disgust but indifference are those who know nothing of death, such as very young children, and doctors and pathologists, whose intellectual curiosity and healing agendas inhibits their disgust at disease.

The opposite is also true: disgust prevents the development of curiosity. If you are repelled by the thought of hyenas, you will never develop an interest in them, nor will you ever discover the truth behind the rumours. Pity works the same way. It is well documented that in the Nazi concentration camps, the absence of shower and toilet facilities caused the inmates to think of themselves as animals and the guards to think of them likewise. It was manifestly less difficult for the Nazis to torture and kill inmates who were covered in filth and excrement. We cannot feel pity for something we loath and abhor, especially when we see it gnawing on a disembodied skull.

Speaking literally, of course, there is nothing particularly dangerous or threatening about feeding on bone, which household dogs do all the time. Bones are waste products, which, as the Hungarian psychiatrist András Angyal explains, 'do not imply obvious noxiousness but merely and essentially *inferiority* and *meanness*. Wastes, to our minds, are something base, and contact with them is experienced as debasing, degrading rather than harmful.'⁹ Beyond that, since bones are no longer 'viable', the idea of reincorporating them into the body seems somewhat perverse.

Not only do hyenas feed on dead bodies, they also sometimes feed on bodies that are, for the moment, still alive. This begs the question whether it is more repellent to eat bodies that are still living or ones that have been dead for so long that only the bones remain. Both acts violate all kinds of social and cultural taboos, including – in the former case – major body envelope violations. Yet plenty of other predators eat this way, including lions, tigers and bears, none of which appears to be an object of widespread revulsion.

Lest we forget, most human beings also feed on dead bodies, which, in order to transform them magically from their original condition, we refer to by such euphemistic terms as 'ham', 'steak', 'sirloin', 'pot roast', 'porterhouse', 'bacon', 'ham' and 'drumstick'. This change of meaning does not come easily to us, however, and in most cases it cannot happen at all. There are very few creatures upon whose bodies the radical act of eating can be performed (mainly cows, sheep, pigs and chickens), and it can never take place with animals that are too close to us (our pets, other humans) or too distant (polar bears, porcupines). One of the criteria for determining whether or not an animal is edible is what that animal feeds on. Most cultures have a strong aversion to eating carnivores, and feeding on scavengers is always taboo.

In this, the hyena fits social anthropologist Mary Douglas's theory that it is their anomalous qualities that lead certain objects or animals to be considered polluting.¹⁰ Her view is based on our tendency to create clear-cut categories for objects in the world, then to project our anxieties on to those things

A striped hyena playing with its keeper.

that cannot be contained by this classification, or that fall in between boundaries. Things that are neither inside nor outside the body, for example, are considered highly repellent – think of spilled blood, excrement, urine or other bodily detritus. Yet, even on a more overt level, hyenas are difficult to categorize for all kinds of reasons. They are neither dog nor cat, neither predator nor scavenger, neither friend nor enemy, but always already a touch of both, making our neat human categories look ridiculous.

Essentially, the hyena has been blighted by the laws of sympathetic magic and contagion, which have been used to account for a wide variety of practices and belief in traditional cultures, and can equally well be applied to our own. The law of contagion, as the nineteenth-century anthropologist J. G. Frazer put it, means that 'things which have once been in contact with each other continue ever afterwards to act on each other';[11] in other words, once is forever. He summarizes the law of similarity as 'like produces like', meaning that resemblance in some properties indicates a fundamental connection or identity.[12] As a scavenger of corpses, then, the hyena, gruesome and uncanny, itself takes on the standing of a corpse. It is the human soul, not the body, that needs protecting from such black magic.

Most people have bad things to say about the hyena, but how many of us have ever seen a hyena in the flesh, or even have a clear sense of what one looks like? The fact is, our impressions of hyenas come from nature documentaries on television, or from *The Lion King*. On wildlife shows, spotted hyenas are invariably presented as cannon fodder, generic extras lurking round the edge of the water hole while the camera seeks out bolder and more telegenic predators, which may well chase hyenas down for a kill.

Hyena postcard, published in 1909 by M. J. Mintz, Chicago. The reverse of the card informs us that the 'Hyena abounds in Central Africa, is nocturnal in its habits, grubbing off corpses, hunting down animals, and in some cases carrying off children.'

And yet, even if it were appropriate to judge non-human animals by human standards, there are certainly plenty of creatures with more questionable habits than the hyena. There are beasts that suck blood, eat excrement, consume their own offspring and spray toxic venom. There are worms that crawl inside the nostrils of their sleeping victims, fish that swim up the urethra and insects that breed in body cavities, none of which is as maligned as the hyena. But there is more at stake here than reputation alone. Conservation researchers argue that only by being aware of our aesthetic prejudices can we set them aside when deciding which animals should be studied and which be saved. Zoological journals are full of papers on leopards, lions and chimpanzees, but animals that are less appealing sometimes get short shrift. There is, admittedly, a huge amount of scientific literature on parasites and other unpopular creatures such as snakes, though much of this research takes place for reasons that have more to do with human medical needs (including the development of antitoxins) than a fascination

Hyena being captured, from the Mastaba tomb of Mereruka (Mera), early 6th Dynasty (2325–2175 BC) section of limestone relief with residual paint from Saqqara.

with the animals in themselves. Those creatures lacking a strong record of 'public relations' often suffer in terms of funding priorities, and this is the certainly true of the hyena. As a result, the brown hyena is close to extinction, and the striped hyena is not far behind.

These days, the main threat to striped hyenas comes from habitat loss, but in the past they were persecuted with impunity. An engraving on the Sixth Dynasty burial tombs at Sakkara depicts a striped hyena on its back, its front and back legs tied together, with a slave stuffing pieces of meat and poultry into its muzzle. In the 1880s, in imperial Russia, a bounty was offered for every striped hyena killed.

There are astonishing accounts of cruelty in Indian hunting and sporting books from the late nineteenth and early twentieth centuries, when hyena baiting was common. The striped hyena was the most frequently baited species, since it is the only type of hyena to be found in this part of the world. The *Illustrated London News* of 9 March 1889 carried a series of drawings entitled 'Hyena Spearing in India', showing colonizers killing striped hyenas for sport, from horseback, as in a polo game. With no foxes to hunt, the Pukka Sahibs in India used hyenas in their cruel games, often on the spurious grounds that the dirty beasts were guilty of stealing children. While such incidents were not unheard of, in this respect striped hyenas were far less guilty than other animals that were rarely hunted down for the crime. Shy and solitary, the striped hyena does not make an especially formidable enemy, but apparently puts up a tough fight when pitted against trained dogs, which it will try to cripple by biting on the legs or neck. If maintained for long enough, a single bite from a hyena can kill a dog on the spot. As a result, bridles were often used on hyenas that had been captured for baiting purposes, so dogs would be less afraid of them. The baiting of striped

Hyena spearing in India, from *The Illustrated London News* (9 March 1889).

A toss & a spill

The loose horse continues the chase

The hyaena speared

hyenas continued to be a common blood sport in the southern Punjab, Kandahar and Ouetta regions of India well into the twentieth century.

In the 1930s it was common for trappers in Turkmenistan, on the borders of Russia, to offer striped hyena skins for sale, advertising them as 'minor quality wolf and fox'. Hyena fur has never been fashionable; still, traps set for other animals, hunted for fur or bush-meat, often cause hyenas to suffer prolonged and painful deaths. Even today, in the border zones between Afghanistan and Pakistan, striped hyenas are regularly trapped or shot by villagers on the grounds that they are a threat to small children sleeping out in the open.

Elsewhere, spotted hyenas continue to be hunted for 'sport'. As mentioned earlier, in *Green Hills of Africa* (1935), Ernest Hemingway recalls how amusing his African guide M'Cola found the spectacle of a hyena shot at close range:

> There was that comic slap of the bullet and the hyena's agitated surprise to find death inside of him. It was funnier to see a hyena shot at a great distance, in the heat shimmer of the plain, to see him go over backwards, to see him start that frantic circle, to see that electric speed that meant he was racing the nickelled death inside him. But . . . the pinnacle of hyenic humor, was the hyena, the classic hyena, that hit too far back while running, would circle madly, snapping and tearing at himself until he pulled his own intestines out and then stood there, jerking them out and eating with relish . . . The hyena was a dirty joke.[13]

Even today, striped hyenas are hunted down and killed whenever children go missing in the Caucuses, Central Asia and Azerbaijan. Again, wolves or bears are more likely to have been the culprits; striped hyenas rarely go after human prey (although they will scavenge human graves, and in some rural areas, stones are placed on burial sites to stop them digging up the bodies).

The hyena's reputation as a violent predator was reinforced by Joanna Greenfield's story published in the *New Yorker* in November 1996. In this account, Greenfield recounts her experience of being attacked and partially eaten by a striped hyena she was looking after in a wildlife refuge in Israel. Although she explains that Efa was a rogue hyena, rescued at birth and raised in captivity, and although she remained fond of Efa and hyenas in general, Greenfield's description of the incident – accompanied by a full-page photo of a particularly mangy-looking hyena (spotted, not striped) – surely served only to confirm the popular impression of this animal as a vile, slavering fiend:

> I lost hope and felt the slowness of this death to be the worst insult. Hyenas don't kill fast, and I could end up in the sand watching my entrails get pulled through a cut in my stomach and eaten like spaghetti, with tugs and jerks . . . By this time, my right arm was a mangled mess of flesh, pushed-out globs of fat, and flashes of bone two inches long . . . trapped in the hyena's mouth, in a tug-of-war like the one I used to play with my dogs – only it was my arm now instead of a sock.[14]

In many parts of Africa, local tribesmen and white ranchers alike blame hyenas for the loss of their livestock, and commonly retaliate with a number of barbaric methods. Some farmers set wire nooses at small openings in the fences of their corrals; once they are caught in the snare, hyenas are then stabbed, clubbed or shot to death. Elsewhere, ranchers will saturate the carcass of a goat or cow with fast-acting poison and leave it for hyenas to feed on during the night. This can result in the deaths of large numbers of animals simultaneously. Such mass poisoning is still widespread in East Africa.[15] Hyenas are now extinct in Mali, and are rapidly disappearing from many other countries in West Africa.

Another major threat to hyenas today (ironically, in the light of the British hyena-starring car crime campaign) is traffic. Like other animals, they are sometimes hit when crossing roads, but hyenas are particularly vulnerable because they feed on road-kill, which puts them directly in the path of oncoming cars. In the middle of the night on a dark highway, such encounters are almost always fatal – for the hyenas, at any rate. Recently, in areas of Namibia where brown hyenas are particularly vulnerable to this kind of accident, road signs have been erected warning drivers to look out for hyenas on the road.

In Afghanistan, Somalia, Ethiopia and other conflict areas, there has been a steep decline in the striped hyena population as a result of landmines, explosives and similar devices. In Israel, where Greenfield was attacked, virtually the entire population of striped hyenas was destroyed when the British government distributed meat contaminated with strychnine in a campaign to wipe out rabies between 1918 and 1948. Although they have largely recovered from this campaign, and are protected by law, the current nature reserves housing them are probably too small to ensure viable populations. Currently, the striped hyena and the brown hyena are both considered 'Near Threatened' by the International Union for Conservation of Nature (IUCN), which maintains a 'Red List' of at-risk and extinct species around the world. The spotted hyena is doing well enough to be considered of 'Least Concern' by IUCN, but its population is also declining, primarily due to habitat loss, and in areas of West Africa spotted hyenas are becoming extinct.

Other endangered animals are protected and bred in zoos, but very few zoos have hyena exhibits. The usual excuse for this is that hyenas sleep during the day, but then, so do big cats and many other creatures that remain popular. The truth is, even though zoos are supposed to be concerned with preservation rather than entertainment, there is little public demand for hyenas. They have never been crowd-pleasers. In fact, when there was only a single striped hyena left in captivity in the US, rather than calling for the animals to be preserved, the Canid/Hyena Advisory Group suggested that, due to the lack of public interest, the animals should be eliminated from zoo populations entirely. This is not entirely unwelcome news to those who understand hyenas. 'Personally', says ecologist Marcus Baynes-Rock, 'I think it is good that hyenas are not being kept in zoos. They need space to be able to get away from higher ranking clanmates, the males need to be able to disperse and they are terrified of humans so it must stress them severely to be stared at all day inside a cage.'[16]

HYENA LOVE

I love hyenas, but I also appreciate that my feelings about them are conflicted. Much of what draws me to this unpopular creature is its uncanny reputation and odd appearance, along with the aura of magic and superstition that surrounds it. Yet my intention in this book, in part, is to show that the hyena's bad rap is undeserved; that hyenas are, in fact, appealing and intelligent animals, much-maligned by centuries of ignorant assumptions. In truth, however, it is not a case of either/or. Hyenas are both smart and scary, both magical and misunderstood. They will never be bunnies or kittens. Even those who spend their lives around them remain wary of their unpredictable nature. Without a doubt, the hyena is a complex creature.

Baby hyena having his breakfast.

Zoo Expressions : No. III., The baby hyena has his breakfast.

While researching this book, I was gratified to discover that I was not alone in my hyena love. Others who are fascinated by hyenas include Berkeley psychology professors Laurence Frank and Stephen Glickman, who first began to study spotted hyenas in the early 1980s in Kenya's Masai Mara National Reserve. In 1985 Frank and Glickman returned to Berkeley with twenty spotted hyena cubs and established a small colony at the University Field Station, nestled in the Berkeley hills. One of Glickman's former students Kay Holekamp – now a professor of Zoology at Michigan State University – has continued to work in the Masai Mara, where she is involved in a long-term behavioural field study of free-living spotted hyenas. After living among the hyenas for over twenty years, Holekamp knows at least 100 animals individually, and is constantly involved in efforts to 'rebrand' this fascinating beast.

Today, the Berkeley hyena colony contains 26 healthy spotted hyenas, each weighing between 130 and 200 pounds. When I

A cute baby hyena.

visited the colony in April 2010, the animals struck me as very friendly; they were placid in disposition and displayed a steady, intelligent gaze. Since most of these hyenas were hand-raised and bottle-fed, they have been and remain on affectionate terms with the field station staff and the students and interns who care for them. The walls of the station are decorated with photographs of the hyenas enjoying games of football and eating pumpkins on Halloween. It was a hot day when I visited, and the hyenas were happily jumping in and out of big tin baths of cold water, splashing together playfully (spotted hyenas apparently love to play in water, and will do so even on cold days). While we stood discussing them, the animals would come and sit nearby, occasionally nuzzling their faces against the fence, hoping to be petted (sadly, this is against the rules).

The Berkeley hyenas are used in experiments and projects designed to test cooperating skills, and they have also been used in research on prostate cancer, human urogenital development and genital anomalies. The National Institute of Mental Health has funded the colony for the last 22 years; unfortunately, however, the grant was recently discontinued. A smaller grant will pay to keep 10 of the 26 hyenas for another four years, but, unless further funding is obtained, most of the Berkeley hyenas will have to be given to zoos.

During my research for this book, I also spent some time with Gregor, a ten-year-old striped hyena at the Living Desert Zoo in Palm Desert, California. Gregor was brought to California from the Estonian Tallinn Zoo at one year old, and apparently has been particularly mellow in disposition since the death of his irritable and moody female partner. Recently, Gregor has begun to paint (or, at least, he has been given paint to play with), and his latest piece sold for $250. And, according to the Auction Network, which sells the paintings in affiliation with the Association of Zoos and Aquariums, Gregor has a particularly expressive style that he creates 'by throwing his whole body into the painting, using his feet, scent rolling on the painting, and licking the canvas'. His work tends to be 'bright and sunny, with lots of yellow squiggles'.

As I noted in the previous chapter, most people these days become familiar with hyenas – the concept of hyenas, at least – by way of *The Lion King*. While the film and subsequent musical played into the hyena's bad reputation, a little further investigation provides reassurance that not all young people have been seduced by the saccharine lies of 'Circle of Life'. The three animated hyenas from the film are also popular characters in fan fiction that celebrates hyenas, occurring in surprising spin-off adventures of their own.

Hyenas also have their followers in the art world. Hyaena Gallery in Burbank, California, describes itself as 'LA's premiere gallery for Dark Art, Lowbrow Art and Outsider Art' and features, among other things, a selection of 'True Crime Artwork and Artifacts'. The gallery also sells illustrations of hyenas by artists like Nik Caesar. Post-punk/goth band Siouxie and the Banshees released an album entitled *Hyaena* in 1984; the music is strange and atmospheric. Hyena Records is a well-known label, and there are many Hyena comedy clubs.

Nik Caesar,
untitled, 2010, pen
and ink drawing.

In a project entitled 'The Hyena Report', artist Dorian Katz uses a child-like style of illustration and fanciful hand lettering in an iridescent palette to present the social and sexual aspects of hyenas through thirteen statements. Alluding to educational articles and children's books, Katz's mixed-media illustrations play with the boundaries between nasty and cute. She is especially interested in the way hyenas have been vilified throughout human history due to the puzzling form of their gendered bodies, leading to various misconceptions and superstitions. According to Katz, 'the hyena's history of marginalization provides numerous parallels with sexual outsider experience in our culture'.

Over the last ten years, there has been a heightened human interest in hyenas, which can only be a good thing for their preservation and general well-being. The Brown Hyena Research Project, based in the southern Namib Desert and led by hyena specialist Dr Ingrid Wiesel, is devoted to tracking and preserving this distinct population of gentle scavengers. Zoologist Aaron Wagner is currently working with striped hyenas in two separate parts of Kenya. The striped hyena, Wagner explains, is one of the few remaining large carnivores whose biology remains poorly understood, and is more seriously endangered than the cheetah, though it receives far less attention (and research funding). A similar research project is under way in south-eastern Turkey, where scientists are monitoring and protecting the last remaining striped hyenas.

Striped hyenas, much easier to catch than the spotted variety, are sometimes imported illegally as pets (footage of big-eared, bottle-feeding babies occasionally turns up on the Internet), but most of them end up in zoos after being discovered and confiscated by the police. This was the fate of Bubbles, a striped hyena found to be living in a neighbourhood backyard in Myrtle

Nik Caesar,
untitled, 2010,
watercolour.

Beach, South Carolina, in August 2009. Bubbles's owner, Nicolas Petcock, was given a ticket for 'harboring a dangerous and vicious animal', and Bubbles was swiftly removed, much to his owner's chagrin. 'He really was a family member to me', lamented the grieving Petcock.

At the time of writing this book, spotted hyenas can be found at 21 zoos in the US and Canada, and striped hyenas in five. Hyenas

Dorian Katz,
The Hyena Report,
2008.

generally do well in captivity; lifespans exceeding 20 years are not uncommon. Spotted hyenas have reached 41 years of age, and brown hyenas 30 years. Despite rumours of financial trouble, the Bronx Zoo has actually added two new animals: the first hyenas in the zoo for 30 years. These twin cubs were born on 3 March 2008 in Denver Zoo, to parents Ngozi and Kibo. The female cub was named Kubwa, Swahili for 'big', and the male Kidogo, Swahili for 'small'. In the Bronx Zoo, they are housed next to the African wild dogs, which are often mistaken for hyenas by visitors.

With its older zoos and longer history of captive breeding, Europe has a better record of preserving the less common species of hyenas. While spotted hyenas can be found in seven different European zoos, there are also five zoos in Europe containing striped hyenas, four that have brown hyenas, and three with aardwolves. Britain is currently the only country where all four species of hyena can be found. These include Dimitri, a hand-reared and apparently well-trained striped hyena currently living at Heythrop Zoological Gardens (hand-raised hyenas, even striped hyenas, may become very tame toward humans, although they are capable of injuring their owners and should be treated carefully). Significantly, Dimitri was one of the hyenas that appeared in the car security campaign in the early 1990s ('Leave it unlocked, and they're laughing') that first introduced me to this fascinating creature.

Finally, just as I was finishing work on this book, I had an unusually close encounter with a spotted hyena in the wild. My partner and I were staying in a tented camp in the Western Serengeti, close to the Grumeti River, where we had recently observed the northern wildebeest migration. Every night, around our camp, we heard the yipping and whooping of spotted hyenas. Shortly before ten o'clock one evening, I was lying awake in bed when I heard a rummaging, snuffling sound, and a large spotted hyena appeared directly in front of the tent opening, about a metre from where I was finishing off a glass of champagne before going to sleep. We stared at one another for a while; in the reflection of electric light, her eyes glowed an eerie red. Unconcerned by my presence, she sniffed around further, then, finding nothing to eat, stood up on her hind legs and noisily drank the water from the portable wash stand at which, an hour or so earlier, I had taken a bath before bed. Again, the hyena proved itself to be a brave and canny scavenger, finding use in what others had left behind. It was rare communion indeed, to share my bathwater with a spotted hyena.

We have always imagined the hyena to be involved with dead bodies, and, as a result, we have convinced ourselves that hyenas are vile, horrible creatures. In mythology and magic, they have been associated with putrefaction and the macabre, with waste and disease. The hyena is the totem animal of the outcast and the taboo, lurking in wastelands, laughing and scavenging. We think about hyenas this way because it is easy to do so, and because we need to have our villains, even in the animal world. But these imagined creatures, almost universally feared and reviled, are a product of human culture, not of nature. Real hyenas, unknown to most of us, are far more diverse and fascinating than the dull, one-dimensional creatures most people think of when they hear the word 'hyena'. Spotted hyenas are courageous and intelligent; striped hyenas are quiet and shy; brown hyenas are bold and sociable; aardwolves are gentle and small. They are all strange and remarkable animals with much to teach us. The hyena's night music may be an unusual melody, but for those who choose to listen, it has a secret splendour all its own.

Timeline of the Hyena

257,000–195,000 BC

Human hairs in fossilized brown hyena dung from South Africa have been identified as dating from this era

1600–1100 BC

Scene of dogs hunting down a hyena appears on an ancient Egyptian papyrus

c. 1125–1290

Hyenas depicted in bestiaries as grave-robbers and corpse-eaters

c. 1526

Leo Africanus describes the hyena as having the legs and feet of a man, in a work translated into English in 1600

1880s–1890s

In imperial Russia, a bounty is offered for every striped hyena killed

Striped hyenas are hunted for sport by horseback colonizers in British India

1900–1910

President Menelik, King of Abyssinia, sends President Theodore Roosevelt a hyena named Bill as a gift

Roosevelt reinforces the reputation of hyenas as 'cowards' in his account of experiences in Africa.

6th century BC	350–300 BC	1st century AD

'The Hyenas', a fable widely credited to Aesop, assumes hyenas are hermaphrodites

Aristotle describes the hyena as a hermaphrodite or sex-changer

Ovid's *Metamorphoses* depicts the hyena as a hermaphrodite

1614	1764–7	c. 1790–1850

Sir Walter Raleigh describes the hyena as the offspring of foxes and wolves

The Beast of Gévaudan terrorizes south-east France. The creature is later suspected to be a rogue striped hyena

Spotted and striped hyenas become popular features of menageries and travelling zoos

1937–8	1950s	2005

Leonora Carrington's 'The Debutante' makes the hyena a popular animal with Surrealists

Spotted hyenas, considered sacred, begin to be fed by the citizens of Harar, Ethiopia. They begin to wander the city streets unharmed

Anonymous photographs of 'hyena men' in Lagos start appearing on the Internet and inspire South African photographer Pieter Hugo to begin his own research

Striped and brown hyenas are declared endangered species

References

INTRODUCTION

1 'Interview with Jannell Cannon', at www.harcourtbooks.com,
   accessed 14 December 2001.
2 Hans Kruuk, *The Spotted Hyena* (Chicago, IL, 1972), p. xiii.

1 EVOLUTION AND DISTRIBUTION

1 'The Hyena', *Harper's New Monthly Magazine*, IX (1854), p. 515.
2 Benny Bleiman, 'Hyena Gals Prefer Suave Foreigners Also',
   Zooillogix Blog (4 September 2007), www.scienceblogs.com/
   zooillogix.
3 Joanna Greenfield, 'Hyena', *New Yorker* (11 November 1996),
   pp. 74–5.
4 Ibid.
5 'The Hyena', p. 515.

2 THE HYENA AND HUMAN HISTORY

1 Strabo, *Geography* [*c.* AD 18], trans. H. L. Jones (Cambridge, MA,
   1924), bk 7, p. 336.
2 Stephen E. Glickman, 'The Spotted Hyena from Aristotle to
   The Lion King: Reputation Is Everything', *Social Research*, LXII/3
   (1995), p. 509.
3 Aristotle, *Historia animalium* [4th century BC], trans. A. L. Peck
   (Cambridge, MA, 1957), vol. VI, pp. 15, 30, 579.
4 Aesop, *Fables*, trans. Olivia Temple and Robert Temple

(Harmondsworth, 1964), p. 341.

5 Ibid., p. 249.

6 Pliny the Elder, *Natural History* [1st century AD], trans.
H. Rackham (Cambridge, MA, 1956), vol. VIII, p. 72.

7 Lucan, *Civil War* [AD 61–65], trans. Edward Ridley (London,
1896), bk 6, pp. 352–4.

8 Clement of Alexandria, 'Paedagogus', in John Boswell, *Christianity,
Social Tolerance and Homosexuality* (Chicago, IL, 1980), p. 356.

9 Anonymous, *Physiologus* [1492], trans. M. J. Curley (Austin, TX,
1979), pp. 52–3.

10 T. H. White, *The Bestiary* (New York, 1960), pp. 30–31.

11 Robert Steele, *Mediaeval Lore from Bartholomew Anglicus* (London,
1905), p. 184.

12 R. Brown, ed., *Leo Africanus, The History and Description of Africa*,
trans. John Pory (London, 1986), p. 947.

13 Edward Topsell, *The History of Four-Footed Beasts and Serpents*
(London, 1607), p. 340.

14 Ibid.

15 Thomas Browne, *Pseudodoxia Epidemica* [17th century], ed. Robin
Robbins (Oxford, 1986), vol. V, p. 241.

16 Walter Raleigh, *History of the World* (London, 1652), bk I, pp.
94–5.

17 Jay M. Smith, *Monsters of the Gévaudan: the Making of a Beast*
(Cambridge, MA, 2011), p. 241.

18 James Bruce, *Travels to discover the source of the Nile in the years
1768, 1769, 1770, 1771, 1772, 1773* (London, 1790), vol. V, pp. 107–120.

19 Sir John Barrow, *An Account of Travels into the Interior of Southern
Africa in the years 1797 and 1798* (London, 1801), vol. I, p. 17.

20 Bruce, *Travels*, Appendix to vol. VII, p. 215.

21 Philip Henry Gosse, *The Romance of Natural History* [1863]
(New York, 1902), p. 48.

22 The source of this description, which recurs in a number of books
of the period, is unknown.

23 J. F. Nott, *Wild Animals: Photographed and Described* (London,
1886), p. 106.

24 W. H. Flower and R. Lydekker, *An Introduction to the Study of Mammals Living and Extinct* (London, 1891), pp. 542–3.

25 Richard Lydekker, *The Royal Natural History* (London, 1893–6), vol. I, p. 492.

26 'Escape of a Hyena from a Menagerie', *Cleveland Weekly Dispatch* (11 February 1858), p. 8.

27 'Hyena Hunt at Coney', *The New York Times* (15 June 1910), p. 12.

28 'Hyena Bit Off Her Finger', *The New York Times* (23 July 1906), p. 7.

29 'Hyena on the Loose', *The New York Times* (9 April 1894), p. 2.

30 'Wild Hyena is at Large', *The New York Times* (16 June 1897), p. 1; 'Hyena Digs up Bodies', *The New York Times* (17 June 1897), p. 1; 'Bullet Ends Hyena's Wanderings', *The New York Times* (22 June 1897), p. 10.

31 E. P. Walker, *et al.*, *Mammals of the World* (London, 1968), vol. XI, p. 1,265.

3 HYENA MAGIC

1 Aristotle, *Historia animalium* [4th century BC], trans. A. L. Peck (Cambridge, MA, 1957), vol. VIII, pp. 28, 25, 92.

2 Pliny the Elder, *Natural History* [1st century AD], trans. H. Rackham (Cambridge, MA, 1956), vol. VIII, p. 72.

3 Ibid., pp. 8, 27–9.

4 D. P. Crandall, 'Himba Animal Classification and the Strange Case of the Hyena', *Africa: The Journal of the International African Institute*, LXXII (2002), p. 309.

5 Alma Gottleib, 'Hyenas and Heteroglossia: Myth and Ritual among the Beng of the Côte d'Ivoire', *American Ethnologist*, XVI (1989), p. 493.

6 Ibid.

7 Aristotle, 'On Marvellous Things Heard', in *The Complete Works of Aristotle* [350–300 BC], ed. Jonathan Barnes (Princeton, NJ, 1984), vol. I, pp. 24–8, 145, 845.

8 Ibid., p. 24.

9 Sir James G. Frazer, *The Golden Bough: A Study in Magic and*

Religion (New York, 1922), p. 190.

10 'The Hyena', *Harper's New Monthly Magazine*, IX (1854), p. 514.

11 Dan Boneh, 'Mystical Powers of Hyenas: Interpreting a Bedouin Belief', *Folklore*, XCVIII (1987), p. 58.

12 Sigmund Freud, *The 'Uncanny'*, standard edn 17 (London, 1919), p. 220.

13 Sigmund Freud, *Totem and Taboo*, standard edn 13 (London 1912), p. 91.

14 Ibid.

15 William Bascom, 'Perhaps Too Much to Chew?', *Western Folklore*, XL (1981), pp. 285–98.

16 Suzanne Pinckney Stetkevych, 'Sarah and the Hyena: Laughter, Menstruation and the Genesis of a Double Entendre', *History of Religions*, XXXVI (1996), pp. 13–41.

17 Ibid.

18 Pliny the Elder, *Natural History*, vol. VIII, pp. 28, 25, 92.

19 Aelian, *On the Characteristics of Animals* [*c.* AD 220–230], trans. A. F. Schofield (Cambridge, MA, 1959), vol. II, bk 6.

20 Allen F. Roberts, *Animals in African Art* (New York, 1995), p. 75.

21 Hagar Soloman, *The Hyena People: Ethiopian Jews in Christian Ethiopia* (Berkeley, CA, 1999), p. 7.

22 Mohammed Adow, 'Taming Ethiopia's Hyenas', BBC One-Minute World News (Monday, 12 April 2004), at www.bbc.co.uk/news, accessed 14 December 2011.

23 A.J.N. Tremearne, 'Nigerian Strolling Players', *Man*, XCV (1914), p. 43.

24 Will Smith, 'The Hyena and Other Men' (2008), at www.museomagazine.com, accessed 14 December 2011.

25 Ibid.

4 WARGS AND SCRUNTS

1 Ovid, *Metamorphoses* [*c.* AD 8], vol. XV, lines 408–9, trans. A. S. Kline, at www.poetryintranslation.com, accessed 14 December 2011.
2 Edmund Spenser, *The Faerie Queene* [1590] (London, 1979), bk 3, line 22.
3 John Lyly, *Euphues: The Anatomy of Wit* [1578] (London, 1916), p. 97.
4 William Shakespeare, *As You Like It* [1623] (New York, 1896), p. 78.
5 John Milton, *Samson Agonistes* [1671] (Cambridge, 1912), p. 748.
6 John Milton, *Pro Se Defensio* [1655] (New Haven, CT, 1971), vol. IV, p. 751.
7 George Chapman, Ben Jonson and John Marston, *Eastward Ho* [1605] (Manchester, 1979), p. 320.
8 John Dryden, *The Conquest of Granada* [1672] (New York, 1910), p. 86.
9 Charlotte Brontë, *Jane Eyre* [1847] (New York, 1902), p. 312.
10 Rudyard Kipling, *The Works of Rudyard Kipling XXVII: The Five Nations, The Years Between, and Poems from History* (London, 1920), p. 56.
11 'When a Burglar Comes In', *Reading Eagle* (20 July 1902), p. 7.
12 Leonora Carrington, *The Debutante* (1937–8). Available at www.redtidebluefire.com, accessed 14 December 2011.
13 Isak Dinesen, *Out of Africa* [1937] (New York, 1992), p. 311.
14 Jannell Cannon, *Pinduli* (New York, 2004).
15 Stephen E. Glickman, 'The Spotted Hyena from Aristotle to *The Lion King*: Reputation Is Everything', *Social Research*, LXII/3 (1995), p. 505.
16 Matt Roth, 'The Lion King: A Short History of Disney-fascism', *Jump Cut*, XL (1996), pp. 15–20.
17 Ibid.
18 'Hyena Committing Suicide', *The New York Times* (23 September 1910), p. 9.
19 Mark Leyner, 'The Hyena King', *Esquire* (1996), p. 164.
20 John Berger, *Ways of Seeing* (London, 1972), p. 19.

1 Marcus Baynes-Rock, personal e-mail communication (8 August 2010).

2 Stephen E. Glickman, 'The Spotted Hyena from Aristotle to *The Lion King*: Reputation Is Everything', *Social Research*, LXII/3 (1995), p. 507.

3 Dan Boneh, 'Mystical Powers of Hyenas: Interpreting a Bedouin Belief', *Folklore*, XCVIII (1987), p. 57.

4 Kay Holekamp, cited in Doug Stewart, 'Africa's Enigmatic Predator', *National Wildlife*, XII (2008), p. 9.

5 Geoffrey Miller, cited in Natalie Angier, 'A Masterpiece of Nature? Yuck!', *The New York Times* (9 August 2010), p. D1.

6 'Instinct in a Hyena', *Harper's New Monthly Magazine*, VI (1853), p. 412.

7 Hans Kruuk, *The Spotted Hyena* (Chicago, IL, 1972), p. 10.

8 'Zoological Proceedings', in Charles Dickens, ed., *Household Words*, VI (1853), p. 377.

9 András Angyal, 'Disgust and Related Aversions', *Journal of Abnormal and Social Psychology*, XXXVI (1941), p. 397.

10 Mary Douglas, *Purity and Danger* [1966] (London, 2002), pp. 167–8.

11 James G. Frazer, *The Golden Bough: A Study in Comparative Religion* (London, 1890), p. 35.

12 Ibid.

13 Ernest Hemingway, *Green Hills of Africa* (New York, 1935), pp. 37–8.

14 Joanna Greenfield, 'Hyena', *New Yorker* (11 November 1996), pp. 74–5.

15 Kay E. Holekamp and L. Smale, 'Human–Hyaena Relations in and around the Masai Mara National Reserve, Kenya', *IUCN SSC Hyaena Specialist Group Newsletter*, V (1992), pp. 19–20.

16 Marcus Baynes-Rock, personal e-mail communication (8 August 2010).

Select Bibliography

Barber, R., *Bestiary* (Woodbridge, 1993)

Barrow, John, *An Account of Travels into the Interior of Southern Africa, in the Years 1797 and 1798* [1801], trans. T. Cadwell and W. Davies (London, 1923)

Berger, John, *Ways of Seeing* (London, 1972)

Buffon, Georges Louis Leclerc, *Natural History, General and Particular*, trans. William Smellie (London, 1791)

Cohen, Martin, *No Holiday: 80 Places You Don't Want to Visit* (New York, 2006)

Dinesen, Isak, *Out of Africa* (New York, 1992)

Douglas, Mary, *Purity and Danger* [1966] (London, 2002)

Flower, William H., and Richard Lydekker, *An Introduction to the Study of Mammals Living and Extinct* (London, 1891)

Frazer, James G., *The Golden Bough: A Study in Comparative Religion* [1890] (London, 1963)

Gosse, Philip Henry, *The Romance of Natural History* [1863] (New York, 1902)

Hemingway, Ernest, *Green Hills of Africa* (New York, 1935)

Hugo, Pieter, and Adetokunbo Abiola, *The Hyena and Other Men* (Munich, 2007)

Kruuk, Hans, *The Spotted Hyena* (Chicago, IL, 1972)

Lucan, *Civil War*, trans. Edward Ridley (London, 1896)

Lydekker, Richard, *The Royal Natural History* (London, 1893–96)

Mauss, Marcel, *A General Theory of Magic* [1950] (London, 2001)

Mezlekia, Nega, *Notes from the Hyena's Belly: An Ethiopian Boyhood* (New York, 2000)

Mills, M.G.L., *Kalahari Hyaenas* (London, 1990)

Nott, John F., *Wild Animals: Photographed and Described* (London, 1886)

Pliny the Elder, *Natural History*, trans. H. Rackham (Cambridge, MA, 1956)

Roberts, Allen F., *Animals in African Art* (New York, 1995)

Roosevelt, Theodore, and Edmund Heller, *Life-histories of African Game Animals* (London, 1915)

Sparrmann, Andreas, *A Voyage to the Cape of Good Hope, towards the Antarctic polar circle, and round the world: But chiefly into the country of the Hottentots and Caffres, from the year 1772 to 1776* (Philadelphia, PA, 1801)

Steele, Robert, *Mediaeval Lore from Bartholomew Anglicus* [1893] (London, 1905)

Topsell, Edward, *The Historie of the Four-Footed Beasts and Serpents* (London, 1607)

Walker, E. P., *et al.*, *Mammals of the World* (Baltimore, MD, 1968)

White, T. H., *The Bestiary* (New York, 1960)

Associations and Websites

BEAST OF GÉVAUDAN
www.betedugevaudan.com

THE BROWN HYENA RESEARCH PROJECT
www.strandwolf.org.za

GUIDE TO HYENAS IN CAPTIVITY
www.species.net/Carnivora/Canidae/GuideHy.htm

IUCN HYAENA SPECIALIST GROUP
www.hyaenidae.org

MARCUS BAYNES-ROCK
www.hararhyenas.wordpress.com

MICHIGAN STATE UNIVERSITY HYENA RESEARCH
www.msuhyenas.blogspot.com

PIETER HUGO
www.pieterhugo.com

RECYCLED BY HYENA
www.recycledbyhyena.com

STRIPES HYENA CONSERVATION
www.msu.edu/~apwagner/conservation.html

Acknowledgements

I would like to thank the following people for sharing with me their experiences of working with hyenas, and for introducing me to a selection of remarkable creatures: Stephen Glickman and Mary Weldele at the University of California, Berkeley, Department of Psychology Field Station; Liz Hile (and Gregor) at the Living Desert Wildlife and Botanical Park in Palm Desert, California; Marcus Baynes-Rock at the Centre for Research on Social Inclusion at Macquarie University; Ingrid Wiesel at the Brown Hyena Research Project in Luderitz, Namibia; and Joshua Monah at African Dream Safaris in Tanzania. At Reaktion Books, I'd like to thank Jonathan Burt, Michael Leaman and Ann Kay. Thanks also, for their thoughts and observations about hyenas, to Gael Belden, Melissa Daum, Mark Dery, Thomas C. Jones and David Sterritt.

Photo Acknowledgements

The author and the publishers wish to express their thanks to the below sources of illustrative material and/or permission to reproduce it.

From Cecil Aldin, *Zoo Babies* (London, 1913): p. 137; photos © The Art Archive: pp. 35 (The Museo di Villa Giulia, Rome), 36 (Musée du Louvre, Paris), 45, 130 (Pyramid of Teti, Saqqara, Egypt); image courtesy of Andrew Beck (www.moyawatenga.co.za): p. 26; Bodleian Library, Oxford: p. 41 (MS Ashmole 1511); The British Library, London (photos © The British Library Board): pp. 40 (Royal MS 12C. xix), 37 (Hartley MS 4751); photo © The Brooklyn Museum: p. 34; Georges-Louis Leclerc, Comte de Buffon, *Histoire naturelle, générale et particulière* (Paris, 1749–88): pp. 48, 50; © Nik Caesar / Bill Shafer & The Hyaena Gallery: pp. 140, 142; © 2005 by Janell Cannon. Reproduced with permission of the author and the Sandra Dijkstra Literary Agency: p. 105; © 2011 Leonora Carrington/Artists Rights Society (ARS), New York: p. 101; from Hugh Craig, ed., *Johnson's Household Book of Nature: Containing Full and Interesting Descriptions of the Animal Kingdom* (New York, 1880): p. 30; photo by A. Cummings: p. 22; © 2012 DenGuy/iStockphoto LP: p. 6; photo courtesy Steve Gorton © Dorling Kindersley: p. 13; photo © Fine Arts Museums of San Francisco: p. 78; from *The Fortean Times* no. 253 (London, 2009): p. 70; courtesy of Richard Goss: p. 138; photo by Carolyn Hilton: p. 120; from Joseph B. Holder, *Our Living World: An Artistic Edition of the Rev. J. G. Wood's Natural History of Animate Creation, Revised and Adapted to American Zoology* (New York, 1885): p. 51; photos © Pieter Hugo (Yossi Milo Gallery, New York): pp. 88, 89, 93; from *The Illustrated London News* (London, 9 March 1889): p. 132; photo by Julia Kalinkina: p. 15; courtesy Dorian Katz (dorian.katz@gmail.com): p. 143; © 1996, Kazuki Takahashi / Konami games: p. 112; courtesy C. M. Kosemen (c.m.kosemen@gmail.com):

p. 11 (bottom); Library of Congress, Washington DC (Prints and Photographs Division): pp. 111, 115, 128; from Richard Lydekker, *The Royal Natural History* (n.p., 1893–6): pp. 53, 57, 67; from Richard Lydekker, *Wild Life of the World* (n.p., 1916): p. 125; from *MAN* XIV (London, 1914): p. 87; from Gaston Maspero, *History of Egypt, Chaldaea, Syria, Babylonia, and Assyria* (London, 1903): p. 96; photo © Metropolitan Museum of Art: p. 74; postcard by M. J. Mintz (Chicago, IL, 1909): p. 129; New York Public Library picture collection: p. 12; from Charles d'Orbigny, *Dictionnaire universel d'histoire naturelle* (Paris, 1849): p. 55; from Manuel Philes, *De animalium proprietate* (*c*. 1533) (photo © The Art Archive): p. 43; courtesy of The Robert Gore Rifkind Center for German Expressionist Studies, Los Angeles County Museum of Art, CA: p. 68; photo © The Michael C. Rockefeller Memorial Collection: pp. 79, 80, 83, 84; photo by Alan Root, Oxford Scientific Films, Ltd (© 1986 World Wildlife Fund for Nature): p. 29; The Royal Library, Copenhagen: p. 37 (Gl. Kgl. S. 1633 4°, Folio 14v); from Isidore Geoffroy Saint-Hilaire, *General and Particular History of Organizational Anomalies in Man and Animals* (Paris, 1832–7): p. 24; from www. scamorama.com/hyena.html: p. 85; from Heinrich Rudolf Schinz, *Naturgeschichte und Abbildungen der enschen und der Saugethiere . . .* (Zurich, 1840): pp. 16, 59, 63, 64, 73, 75; from Johann Christian Daniel Schreber, *Die Säugthier in Abbildungen nach der Natur mit Beschreibungen* (Erlangen, 1775): p. 60; from *Scientific American Supplement* 508 (September 26, 1885): p. 11 (top); illustration by Deborah Simon: p. 54; © Sinauer Associates, 2001: p. 19; photo by Jill Sneesby, J&B Photographers, www.jandbphotographers.com: p. 27; Staatliches Museum Schwerin, Berlin: p. 49; © 2011 The Andy Warhol Foundation for the Visual Arts, Inc. / Artists Rights Society (ARS), New York: p. 104; illustration by Una Fricker, © 1996 Wizards of the Coast llc: p. 113 (right); illustration by Basil Wolverton: p. 106; photos © Zoological Society of London: pp. 44 (from Edward Topsell, *The Historie of Foure-footed Beastes* [London, 1607]), 46 (from William Cornwallis Harris, *Portraits of the Game and Wild Animals of Southern Africa* [London, 1840]), 94 (from The Rev. J. G. Wood, *The Illustrated Natural History* [London 1861–3]), 100 (from Pierre Boitard, *Le Jardin des Plantes: description et mœurs des mammifères de la Ménagerie et du Muséum d'Histoire Naturelle* [Paris, 1842]).

Index